Law, Religion, and Public Policy

Law, Religion, and Public Policy

A Commentary on First Amendment Jurisprudence

Julia K. Stronks

LEXINGTON BOOKS

A division of
ROWMAN & LITTLEFIELD PUBLISHERS, INC.
Lanham • Boulder • New York • Toronto • Plymouth, UK

LEXINGTON BOOKS

A division of Rowman & Littlefield Publishers, Inc.
A wholly owned subsidiary of The Rowman & Littlefield Publishing Group, Inc.
4501 Forbes Boulevard, Suite 200
Lanham, MD 20706

Estover Road
Plymouth PL6 7PY
United Kingdom

British Library Cataloguing in Publication Information Available

Library of Congress Cataloging-in-Publication Data

Stronks, Julia K.
Law, religion, and public policy : a commentary on first amendment jurisprudence / Julia K. Stronks.
p. cm.
Includes bibliographical references and index.
ISBN: 978-0-7391-0312-8
1. Freedom of religion—United States. 2. United States. Constitution. 1st Amendment
I. Title.

KF4783 .S77 2001
342.73'0852—dc21

2001050509

Printed in the United States of America

™ The paper used in this publication meets the minimum requirements of American National Standard for Information Sciences—Permanence of Paper for Printed Library Materials, ANSI/NISO Z39.48–1992.

For Matthew

When you asked, "Mom, why do people sue each other?"
I answered, "Probably because they don't understand each other."
You then replied, "Well, I think they should listen harder."
I agree.

Contents

Preface

Many years ago when I first was practicing law, I had a client who was accused of violating several state statutes. His defense was that he was practicing his religion. As I researched his case, I discovered that the law wasn't really very clear about what was and what wasn't religious activity. Then, when I discussed the case at pretrial with the judge, the judge said, "I am a religious man. I know what religion is, and your client doesn't have it." We settled the case, but years later I remain grateful to both that client and the judge for putting me on this path of inquiry—in law, what does it mean to be religious?

I am also grateful to scholars whose work I know but whom I have met only briefly: MaryAnn Glendon, Michael McConnell, Douglas Laycock, Michael Sandel and Jean Bethke Elshtain. These scholars have led the way for those of us thinking about the role of faith in public life and they continue to challenge the public at large to consider the appropriate task of government.

As I write this preface the Supreme Court has just handed down its decision in a school prayer case that originated in Santa Fe, Texas. Forty years after *Engle v Vitale* we are still debating whether and how students can pray at school functions. The case highlights the necessity of a book like this. The young woman that prayed over the microphone at a high school football game is certain that the government tried to limit her freedom of religion. By stopping public prayer, the school was substituting a faith of secularism for her faith in God. The school, on the other hand, believed that stopping public prayer was substituting a faith-neutral policy for a religious activity. They disagreed about the nature of religion, the nature of religious activity and the notion of what it means to be secular.

Introduction

As we enter the twenty-first century, much political debate in the United States considers the nature of civil society. Legal scholars and political commentators like MaryAnn Glendon, Jean Bethke Elshtain, Michael Sandel, William Bennett and others challenge us to think about the sort of institutions that are necessary in a healthy, pluralistic, self-governing community. One part of this discussion concerns the relationship between faith and politics in a liberal democracy:

- Should the Ten Commandments be placed in the public school? (The U.S. House of Representatives said yes.)
- Should evolution be the only origin of life perspective taught in the public school? (The Kansas state board of education said no.)
- How should government interact with faith groups that preach hatred? (Cities across the country are constantly revising their approach to this issue.)

All of these topics have one thing in common—they force us to think about how government and religion should interact.

Philosophers Robert Audi and Nicholas Wolterstorff articulate the parameters of this public debate in the recent *Religion in the Public Square*. Audi argues that religion and politics should be separate. He takes a "neutrality" position saying that liberal democracy requires the state to tolerate religion and to be impartial to it. He goes further to say that the implication of neutrality is that citizens have an obligation to use secular reasons in their support for public policy. This is because the liberal state's job is to accommodate people regardless of their individual preferences for a certain type of life. Coercion by the state must occur only when civic order is at stake—it must be grounded in reasons that "any rational adult citizen can endorse as sufficient."[1] These reasons, to Audi, are clearly only those that are secular.

Wolterstorff, on the other hand, argues that religion and politics should not be separated. Government does have the obligation to be impartial toward beliefs, but this does not mean that citizens have to impose epistemological restraint on their support for or against public policies. Wolterstorff's vision emphasizes that the government's job is to do justice, but in our discussion about what justice is, we all are allowed to bring our perspectives to the table. Government must be impartial to religious belief but it must not be required to be separate from religious belief.

The disagreement between Audi and Wolterstorff is in part disagreement about the role of government, but it also stems from a disagreement about the nature of and the role of religious belief. This book explores the relationship between our legal culture's perspective of religion and our approach to the notion of *neutrality* when we talk about religious freedom. I examine American judicial interpretation of the First Amendment religion clauses and suggest that much of our disagreement about the role of government in these cases stems from our inconsistent use of words like *religious* and *secular*. The First Amendment to the U.S. Constitution requires that "Congress shall make no law respecting an establishment of religion, or prohibiting the free exercise thereof." However, interpreting this clause requires an understanding of what religion is.

Religion in the United States is an emotion-packed topic. It affects public policy matters from public schools to medical research to taxes. Recent analyses indicate that nondenominational American churches are experiencing a "return to religion" in record numbers, and the nationwide growth of interest in "spirituality" suggests that Americans are looking for something that addresses fundamental questions in life.

However, with this new interest in the spiritual and religious aspect of life comes a heightened awareness of a particular problem. The First Amendment religious protection policies of the United States government, particularly as expressed by the Supreme Court, have not given Americans sufficient guidance in resolving conflicts that involve freedom of religion claims. What do we do if all doctors in a public hospital refuse to administer abortions because the procedures conflict with their religion? How do we handle the rights of families to control the medical aspects of their children's lives when the children are dangerously ill? Does the war on drugs justify the prohibition of hallucinogenic substances used in religious sacraments?

Americans *believe* that we tolerate great religious diversity. We boast of religious pluralism as evidenced by the more than 1,200 different religious bodies that co-exist in the United States. We hold the concepts *freedom of religion*, *governmental neutrality toward religion* and the *separation of church and state* as examples for the world to follow. However, despite Americans' belief that tolerance and government neutrality toward religions dominate the political arena, First Amendment jurisprudence is in flux and is constantly under attack. Constitutional scholars decry the incoherence and instability of First Amendment theory, and, despite 200 years of First Amendment jurisprudence, many groups still claim to be discriminated against on the basis of their religion. Although the United States Supreme Court has made numerous decisions concerning the implication and application of the First Amendment, these decisions have been of little help in answering the questions: what *is* religious activity, and how far will we as a nation go to protect it?

The Supreme Court has held that the government may not establish a religion, nor may it establish a religion of secularism. However, the meaning of this directive is not clear unless religion and secularism are defined. In many cases, courts indicate that secularism exists when hostility to religion is exhibited. However, in curriculum cases, for example, another approach comes to light. Some litigants do argue that schools violate their First Amendment religious freedom rights when books or curricula present ideas that conflict with their religious beliefs. But other litigants take the argument in a different direction. They say that secularism itself is a faith. As such, if it is part of a curriculum in a public school, it violates the First Amendment.

This argument highlights a struggle that the Supreme Court has been involved in over a period of time. In the 1890 case *Davis v Beason*, the Court said that religion was involved when one made reference to God or a deity.[2] This is referred to as the *Davis* definition of religion. But, in 1967, the Court held that atheists were allowed to claim the religious conscientious objector status under federal law, because atheism was considered to be a view that reflected an "ultimate commitment" that functioned as a religion.[3] This is referred to as the *Seeger* definition of religion. So, does religion involve concepts like God, salvation, sin, prayer and so forth? Or, is religion any ultimate value about humanity that functions as a faith commitment (including secularism)? The difference is important because it forms the foundation of the debates that make up modern-day religious freedom disputes.

This book explores the assumptions that judges bring to their decisions as they define religion. Part I looks at 200 years of judicial interpretation. What guidance has the Supreme Court given us as we have struggled to think about the meaning of the First Amendment? Are concepts like *accommodationism* or *separation of church and state* really very helpful in this discussion?

Part II explores specific policy areas. It considers the beliefs that judges hold about religion when they are asked to define religion in applying the First Amendment to public policy problems, and it examines in detail the impact of judicial decisions about religion on three public policy areas:

> *Curriculum wars*: What assumptions do judges bring to their cases when they try to determine which public school courses have an inappropriately "religious" (as opposed to moral, philosophical or ideological) foundation.

Regulation of employment decisions by religious institutions: Title VII of the 1964 Civil Rights Act prohibits employers from discriminating. However, under a religious freedom exemption to this act a Christian institution does not have to hire a Muslim. Now, in applying this exemption, how do the courts determine which belief systems are adequately "religious" to qualify? And, how do the judges know when "religious discrimination" has occurred (as opposed to gender discrimination, for example).

Public aid to private institutions: When federal money goes to private institutions, how do courts separate what is permissibly political or charitable from what may be impermissibly religious? Does President Bush's emphasis on government partnership with faith-based institutions violate the First Amendment?

An assessment across the policy areas of curriculum, employment decisions by religious institutions, and government partnership with social service agencies reveals a number of themes. Both "religion" and "religious activity" mean different things to different judges. Even more diverse, however, are the judges' perceptions about the implication of religion for the rest of life. Some judges believe that religion can be separated from public life. They argue that religion is private; government policy must be nonreligious or neutral. Other judges suggest that belief systems, including religion, necessarily define adherents' economic, family and educational lives. They say religion cannot be separated from the rest of life. Still others are completely unaware of their assumptions, which makes for decisions that contain internally inconsistent holdings.

Part III of the book examines prevailing religious freedom theories, asking whether or not scholars have provided sufficient guidance to judges in their struggle with balancing the establishment clause of the First Amendment against the free exercise clause. It considers the implication of using different understandings of the nature of religious belief, and then it takes one philosopher's approach to religion and applies it to the policy areas examined in part II.

The extent to which religious freedom is protected in a society is more than just a legal problem. Religious tolerance is achieved only when all segments of society—employers, landlords, schools and so forth—acknowledge it as important. However, the definition of "religion" is something that has been left up to the courts in this country. Even when legislation specifically endorses religious tolerance, the questions "What is religion, and which religions are protected?" are addressed primarily by the judicial process. Scholars and judges admit that the judicial treatment of religion is "inconsistent," "unworkable" and "not grounded in history."[4] My argument is that much of our confusion about the parameters of religious freedom stems from our failure to carefully examine our various assumptions about the definition of religion. What assumptions do judges bring to their definitions? Do the definitions reveal a cultural bias that hurts some groups of people, or is the problem deeper than this?

Notes

1. Robert Audi and Nicholas Wolterstorff, *Religion in the Public Square: The Place of Religious Convictions in Political Debate* (Lanham, Md.: Rowman & Littlefield, 1998) 17.

2. *Davis v Beason,* 133 U.S. 333 (1890).

3. *U.S. v Seeger,* 380 U.S. 163 (1965).

4. Michael McConnell, "Neutrality Under the Religion Clauses," *Northwestern University Law Review* 81 (1986): 146; Mark Tushnet, "The Constitution of Religion," *Connecticut Law Review* 18 (1986): 701; MaryAnn Glendon, "Structural Free Exercise," *University of Michigan Law Review* 90 (1991): 477.

Part One

The Problem

Chapter One

Two Hundred Years of Jurisprudential Mess

In 1993, the United States Supreme Court handed down three religious freedom cases that found in favor of the parties asserting the need for protection of their faiths. The outcome of these cases was somewhat of a surprise in academic and legal circles because in 1990 the Court had issued a sweeping opinion that undercut thirty years of developing "religious freedom" protection. The surprise and unease of the legal community grew during the summer of 1994 as the Court handed down a decision that not only found against the arguments of a religious community, but seemed to contradict one of the 1993 decisions.

On one hand, this wavering of the Court has been surprising. On the other hand, for decades scholars have characterized the Supreme Court's religious freedom jurisprudence as inconsistent, claiming that by fashioning Constitutional tests that have little grounding in history, giving little guidance to legislatures, the Court has politicized the religion clauses of the First Amendment in a way that results in discrimination to particular groups of people. Even the judges themselves criticize their own decisions. As Justice Antonin Scalia has scathingly observed,

> [o]ur cases interpreting and applying the [religion clauses] have made such a maze . . . that even the most conscientious governmental officials can only guess what motives will be held unconstitutional. We have said essentially the following: Government may not act with the purpose of advancing religion, except when forced to do so by the Free Exercise Clause (which is now and then); or when eliminating

> existing governmental hostility to religion (which exists sometimes); or even when merely accommodating governmentally uninhibited religious practices, except that at some point (it is unclear where) intentional accommodation results in the fostering of religion, which is of course unconstitutional.[1]

It is undisputed that our courts are inconsistent in their treatment of religion, but the question is, why has this occurred? Are the judges simply capricious in their decisions, or is there a flaw in the approach that they take in their decision-making?

Of the three religious freedom cases handed down by the Supreme Court in 1993, in only one did the judges address the nature of religion. In *Church of the Lukumi Babalu Aye v Hialeah* the Court had to assess the constitutionality of a Florida city's statute that prohibited the sacrifice of animals.[2] The Court's decision focused on the intent of the statute, simply assuming that the Santerian petitioners were religious. The Santerian faith teaches that every person has a destiny which is fulfilled with the "aid and energy of the orishas [spirits]."[3] The foundation of the faith is the development of a personal relationship with the spirits which is accomplished, in part, through animal sacrifice. The Court assumed that this was religious activity, saying only

> [t]he city does not argue that Santaria [sic] is not a "religion" within the meaning of the First Amendment. Nor could it. Although the practice of animal sacrifice may seem abhorrent to some, "religious beliefs need not be acceptable, logical, consistent, or comprehensible to others in order to merit First Amendment protection."[4]

The Court's summary treatment of this issue foundational to the holding of the case suggests that the definition of religion is not really a question anymore. This part of the book examines the Supreme Court decisions that have asked the question, "What is and what is not religious activity?" The first section of chapter one illustrates how the Court's definition of religion developed. It explores the Supreme Court's move from a content-based definition of religion focusing on belief in God, to a functional approach focusing on Paul Tillich's concept of "ultimate meaning." The second section illustrates the problem that federal courts run into when they try to apply the Supreme Court's definitions.

Defining Religion

Over the course of religious freedom jurisprudence, the Supreme Court claims to have recognized that people's ability to act in accordance with their belief underlies the fundamental right of religious freedom. The Court's decisions have acknowledged that the right to religious freedom extends to conduct as well as belief. But, it is the *legal* definition of religion that first determines when the

First Amendment is invoked; if a litigant's perspective is not religious, the First Amendment protections do not apply. Therefore, the definition of religion is fundamental to the jurisprudence. This definition can be substantive, or it can be functional. Both approaches have troublesome aspects.

Substantive, or content-based, definitions determine that people are religious or nonreligious on the basis of the substance of their beliefs. Law professor Stanley Ingber points out that unfortunately, attempts to define religion by reference to God or other aspects of faith result in arguments about Truth that judges cannot resolve. Because content-based definitions exclude beliefs that are unfamiliar to judges, not only can they exclude certain faiths, but they can also allow judges to second-guess the centrality or particular tenets of a faith.[5] Nonmainstream religions may suffer discrimination because of their unorthodoxy, but adherents of mainstream religions that interpret sections of the Bible or the Talmud differently than do the judges may also be left out.[6]

Functional definitions, on the other hand, avoid inquiry into the content of belief. People are religious or nonreligious based on how their beliefs function in their life. However, such an all-encompassing definition has problems of its own. As the following cases illustrate, if religion is that which deals with "fundamental questions" or "ultimate values" all perspectives are arguably religious.

Despite the debate and the compromises that surrounded the religion clauses of the First Amendment prior to its ratification, very little litigation developed the Amendment until the twentieth century. The religion clauses were not made incumbent on the states until the mid-1940s, so it is not surprising that until 1950 only three or four cases offered any guidance as to what religion is and what it is not.

The earliest Supreme Court cases suggest that the definition of religion should be substantive. In 1890, in *Davis v Beason,* the Court required that religion refer to belief in and worship of a deity.

> The term 'religion' has reference to one's views of his relations to his Creator, and to the obligations they impose of reverence for his being and character, and of obedience to his will . . . The first amendment . . . was intended to allow every one under the jurisdiction of the United States to entertain such notions respecting his relations to his Maker.[7]

By the 1960s, however, the judicial definition of religion was refocused so that the emphasis was no longer on the substance of belief, but rather on the life of the believer: in what way does the belief affect the life led by the believer?

This transition is illustrated most clearly by the 1961 case *Torcaso v Watkins* when the Court invalidated a provision of a Maryland law that required public officials to declare a belief in God. The Court spoke of religion based on other than a belief in God holding that

> neither a State nor the Federal Government can constitutionally force a person "to profess a belief or disbelief in any religion." Neither can constitutionally pass laws or impose requirements which aid all religions as against non-believers, and neither can aid those religions based on a belief in the existence of God as against those religions founded on different beliefs.[8]

In a footnote the Court added that among "religions" which do not teach what would generally be considered a belief in God were Buddhism, Taoism, Ethical Culture and Secular Humanism. Implied is a comprehensive view of religion. The groundwork is laid for the view that religion is a commitment to a particular definition of reality, the nature of humanity and people's place in the world. The distinction between secular and religious begins to blur.

By 1965, the Court refocused its approach to religion, turning away from a substantive approach to defining religion in order to advocate a functional approach. In *United States v Seeger,* the Court criticized the congressional exemptions set forth in the Universal Military Training and Service Act. The Act had called for belief in a Supreme Being as a prerequisite to conscientious objector status. According to the Court, however, the only legitimate issue to be considered when assessing religious belief was "whether the beliefs professed by a registrant are sincerely held and whether they are, in his own scheme of things, religious."[9] In addressing the issue of a Supreme Being the Court said that some people believe in a purely personal God, some in a supernatural deity; others think of religion as a way of life envisioning as its ultimate goal the day when all men can live together in peace. All these approaches were to be considered religions. The courts were not allowed to determine the validity of a claimant's vision of truth or to question the existence of his or her Supreme Being.

However, at the same time, the Court said that those beliefs which were based on a "merely personal moral code" were not allowed exemption from the draft. The only definition of moral code the Court gave was that which was not related to a Supreme Being. The Court then further confused the issue by citing approvingly Paul Tillich's assertion that if the word *God* has no meaning for an individual, *God* could be the same as that belief which an individual had regarding the "source of your being, of your ultimate concern, of what you take seriously without any reservation."[10] The difference between this and a moral, personal code was never made clear.

Unfortunately, this distinction between religion and moral codes becomes critical to both free exercise and establishment clause jurisprudence. Moreover, the *Seeger* standard suggests that if religion is a way of life, it defines a person's approach to life. Does this mean that in a broad sense, all of this person's activity becomes religious?

Despite the unanswered questions that the *Seeger* test engendered, in *Welsh v United States* the Court affirmed the functional approach by citing its *Seeger* test, noting

> [t]he reference to the registrant's own scheme of things was intended to indicate that the central consideration in determining whether the registrant's beliefs are religious is whether these beliefs play the role of a religion and function as a religion in the registrant's life.[11]

In both *Welsh* and *Seeger* the Court permitted exemption from the draft for free exercise claimants after the Court determined that their beliefs were religious in nature. The Court did this despite the fact that several claimants maintained that their objections were not, to them, "religiously" based. Then, in 1971, the Court contradicted itself by upholding a federal law that arguably favored pacifistic religions over those that distinguished between wars. In *Gillette v United States* the Court determined as constitutional the section of the Universal Military Training and Service Act that exempted those who opposed all wars from military service.[12] The Act withheld the exemption from men who opposed only unjust wars or who analyzed individual conflicts case by case determining the morality of each. It is clear that the legislators and judges were distinguishing between belief systems—but the criteria for the distinctions are not clear.

Together, these cases raise difficult issues: Does the First Amendment permit legislators to distinguish between religious and nonreligious persons? What is a nonreligious person? May lawmakers create laws that distinguish between different religions? And what of those laws that appear to apply to all persons equally but have a disparate effect on persons of a particular religion?

Immediately problems emerge. Despite the broad definition of religion in *Seeger*, the Court's insistence on the possibility of *nonreligion*, and the distinction between morals and religion, forces other courts to draw lines in constitutional jurisprudence. Which types of beliefs will the First Amendment protect?

The Court has not advanced further discussion of the nature of religion since the days of the military conscientious objector cases. However, since the 1960s, several lower federal courts have picked up where the Supreme Court left off. These cases are presented here.

Several of these cases illustrate the lengths to which a court will go to protect minority groups from a majoritarian perspective of religion. However, at the same time, they illustrate that the definition of religion involves not just determining what groups to include, but also what type of activity is religious rather than secular.

In the first case the court used the *Seeger* test to declare a group's belief to be religious, despite the argument of the group that it had a secular perspective. In the next case, the same circuit court judge relied on the *Seeger* definition but declared the claimant's perspective on life to be nonreligious. The third case shows a judge admitting that the claimants were religious but declaring that their particular activity was not an important part of their religion. In the last case the court assumed the neutrality of the public school system and refused to deal with the claimant's argument that the activity of the government was religious in character.

Transcendental Meditation

The judge most active in developing the Supreme Court's definition of religion is Judge Adams of the Third Circuit Court of Appeals. In the 1979 case *Malnak v Yogi*, the Third Circuit held that Transcendental Meditation (TM) was a religion, and therefore could not be taught in the public schools.[13] This ruling was over the express objection of the defendants who claimed that their teaching was a secular mental exercise.

Judge Adams concurred with the majority opinion, but he took the opportunity to develop a definition of religion that drew from *Seeger* and *Torcaso*. Adams said that religion existed when a belief system was one of ultimate concerns that addressed issues like life and death, and people's role in the universe. The belief system also had to be comprehensive. And, if it had the traditional cloak of religion (prayer, ritual and so forth) the case for religious activity was made. Adams cautioned that the traditional elements of religion did not have to exist, but their presence was determinative.

When applied to TM and the Science of Creative Intelligence, the test resulted in a finding of religion:

> Creative Intelligence, according to the textbook in the record, is "at the basis of all growth and progress" and is, indeed, "the basis of everything." Transcendental Meditation is presented as a means for contacting this "impelling life force" so as to achieve "inner contentment." Creative Intelligence can provide such "contentment" because it is "a field of unlimited happiness," which is at work everywhere and visible in such diverse places as in "the changing of the seasons" and "the wings of a butterfly."[14]

On the issue of comprehensiveness, the court said

> The Science of Creative Intelligence provides answers to questions concerning the nature both of world and man, the underlying sustaining force of the universe, and the way to unlimited happiness. Although it is not as comprehensive as some religions—for example, it does not appear to include a complete or absolute moral code—it is nonetheless sufficiently comprehensive to avoid the suggestion of an isolated theory unconnected with any particular world view or basic belief system.[15]

Judge Adams found the mantra of TM to be sufficiently ceremonial to clinch the definitional issue.

Adams is to be commended for his effort to deal carefully with the difficult issue of definition. However, within five years he amended his approach.

Personal and small group religions

In 1981, in the case *Africa v Pennsylvania*, the Third Circuit Court of Appeals tried to implement the functionalist approach of the *Seeger* court, and the defined approach of Judge Adams in *Malnak.*[16]

Frank Africa was a "Naturalist Minister" of a group named MOVE. At the time of the suit he was a prisoner claiming that the state violated his right to religious freedom because it refused to provide him with the special diet of raw food required by his religion. The District Court and the Court of Appeals both held that the group MOVE was not a religion, and thus, Africa was not entitled to any First Amendment consideration for his claim. The courts relied on the broad, functional approach to defining religion set forth in *Seeger*, but the judges' own assumptions about religion direct the way that the *Seeger* standards are applied.

The MOVE religion was characterized by Africa and other witnesses as involving the following:

- MOVE's goals were to bring about absolute peace, to stop violence and all that is corrupt;
- there was no governing hierarchy because all members were equal;
- adherents were committed to a natural, moving, generating way of life and thus, to eat anything other than raw food would be in violation of the religion;
- there were no distinct ceremonies or rituals because every act of life was invested with religious meaning or significance;
- every time a MOVE person opened his or her mouth, church was held.

The court determined that it had to find three conditions for a religion to exist. The beliefs would be religious in nature if they addressed "fundamental and ultimate" questions having to do with "deep and imponderable matters." Second, a religion is comprehensive in nature; it consists of a "belief system" as opposed to an "isolated teaching." Third, a religion could be recognized by external signs. However, an adjustment to Judge Adams's *Malnak* definition is at work here. Adams now says

> the free exercise clause does not protect all deeply held beliefs, however "ultimate" their ends or all-consuming their means. An

> individual or group may adhere to and profess certain political, economic, or social doctrines, perhaps quite passionately. The first amendment, though, has not been construed, at least as yet, to shelter strongly held ideologies of such a nature, however, all-encompassing their scope.[17]

As many scholars have argued, this case is troublesome because the three conditions reflect a particular cultural approach that defines "religion" as that which contains elements found in mainstream American religions.[18] Moreover, in finding that MOVE did not meet the three conditions, the court gave little credence to testimony that addressed these issues in concepts unfamiliar to the justices. For example, the court first ruled that MOVE did not address deep and imponderable matters despite the testimony that the perspective gave the adherents a system by which to determine right from wrong and good from evil.

> MOVE is absolutely opposed to all that is wrong . . . we believe in using things [but] not misusing things . . . the air is first, but pollution is second. Water is first, but poison is second. The food is first, but the chemicals that hurt the food are second . . . We believe in the first education, the first government, the first law.[19]

The court also said that MOVE was not a belief system in that it was not comprehensive. Adherents had testified that the MOVE religion was "total"; it encompassed every aspect of MOVE members' lives; there was "nothing that is left out." However, in the court's opinion this was not sufficiently life encompassing.

Finally, the court listed signs by which a religion could be recognized: services, ceremonies, clergy, proselytizing, observance of holidays and other similar manifestations associated with the traditional religions. The court held that MOVE failed to exhibit any of these elements even though the court's description of MOVE included the group's perspective of its holidays, ceremonies and hierarchical structure, and the group testified that one goal was to revolutionize the world to its view. The court focused on MOVE's lack of specific holidays or scriptures.

The court's finding that MOVE was not a religion hinged on factors which indicated MOVE was unlike most American religions.[20] The fact that any definition of religion involves the preconception of those creating the definition is illustrated in *Africa*. This is problematic not only because it opens the door to judicial bias, but also because it results in inconsistent decisions.

The religious adherents will not always lose out. Over the past fifteen years, lower courts have used Judge Adams's approach or the *Seeger* approach to find Scientology, witchcraft and Krishna Consciousness to be religions. Unfortunately, the courts' decisions are very conclusory. For example, in *Dettmer v Landon* the court said that witchcraft was a religion because the adherents believed in another world and had a concern for improving the life of others.[21] Its ceremonies paralleled other traditional religions. Therefore, witchcraft was religious. The problem is that we still do not really know what religion is. Was there really such a difference in the "religiousity" of the MOVE adherents on one hand and TM or witchcraft adherents on the other?

Mixing races

The effect that civil rights statutes have on sectarian schools is an area of the law that is in flux. One federal court has held that 42 USC sec 1981 prohibits private schools from excluding children because of their race. In *Brown v Dade Christian School, Inc.*, parents brought a federal lawsuit against a church operated school after being informed that their children were refused admission because they were black.[22] The Fifth Circuit Court of Appeals was faced with a free exercise claim when the school asserted that intermingling of races was in violation of its religious tenets.

The court considered whether the school's defense was actually based on a religious belief and concluded that free exercise was not an issue because the religion did not really include separating the races as an element. This conclusion was based on the court's perception that the school as an institution and the church it was affiliated with did not have a clearly articulated policy of segregation. The court said that it did not require the school to have the policy in writing, but the fact that the policy was not included in the literature about the school seemed determinative.

The principal and pastor had testified that enrolling blacks would constitute disobedience to the Bible. Testimony showed that the church believed integration of races was against Biblical authority as set forth in the stories of the Tower of Babel, the confusion of tongues in Acts and God's dealing with the nation of Israel. Despite this, the court found that segregation was not a *religious* belief and refused to allow even a hearing on the First Amendment issue. In the court's opinion, the belief was one of social policy or philosophy, not religion.

One of the concurring judges, Justice Goldberg, wrote a separate opinion cautioning the court against judicial policy that discriminates against small groups that have yet to articulate their beliefs fully. He said that the plurality opinion of the Court illustrated how "findings of fact" on religious issues may hide a value-laden assumption about what religion really is. Judge Goldberg believed that the discriminatory admissions policy was based on religious conviction, but he then went on to say that this particular tenet of the faith was "not central to their faith." Moreover, this judge believed that integration of the races, "although constituting disobedience to God, would not endanger salvation."[23] Thus, it was a minor element. He concurred with the court's decision that the school should be enjoined from barring other races.

When courts assess the sincerity of a claimant's religious belief the inquiries can become a tool to impose a majoritarian view of what a religious practice is or should be.

Creation science

In 1982 an Arkansas "equal time" statute mandated that "Public schools within this State shall give balanced treatment to creation science and to evolution-science." The constitutionality of the statute was successfully challenged in *McLean v Arkansas Board of Education* on the theory that by teaching creation science the law established a religion in the school. The federal district court hearing the case in Arkansas focused its analysis on the allegation that creation science is a religious belief.

Proponents of the equal time statute had argued that two positions exist which attempt to explain the origins and development of the earth and life: creation and evolution. They argued that evolutionary theory is, like scientific creationism, an explanation of the origin of humanity. It is based upon presupposed naturalistic processes, such as mutation and natural selection. Both scientific creationism and evolutionary theories can be considered "scientific" in that they explore natural phenomena. But, both can be called "religious" because they entail a foundational or pre-theoretical commitment—a commitment without the benefit of conclusive scientific evidence—to assumptions concerning the development of life. Because evolution expressed a religious perspective in the broad sense of the term, excluding creation science from the classroom violated both the establishment clause and the free exercise rights of those who rejected evolution. The statute was the legislators' attempt to balance the score.

The *Seeger* definition of religion lends support to the proponents' argument. Evolution arguably provides a comprehensive explanation of life and reality, and what it means to be human. However, the court dismissed the argument that evolution could be a religion in one paragraph concluding that the argument had no legal merit.

> [I]t is clearly established in the case law, *and perhaps also in common sense*, that evolution is not a religion and that teaching evolution does not violate the Establishment Clause.[24]

Is the court's refusal to consider the religious aspect of evolution reflective of a majoritarian consensus? Is there a religious aspect not only to evolutionary theory, but to any scientific theory? In one analysis of the *McLean* case, law professor David Caudill explains that philosophers of science have consistently recognized that natural science is founded on an aspect of faith or a belief in certain presuppositions—belief in the scientific enterprise itself. He cites Michael Polanyi, who in *Science, Faith and Society* said:

> The premises of science on which all scientific teaching and research rests are the beliefs held by scientists on the general nature of things. The influence of these premises on the pursuit of discovery is great and indispensable. They indicate to scientists the kind of questions which seem reasonable and interesting to explore, and the kind of conceptions and relations that should be upheld as possible, even when some evidence seems to contradict them, or that, on the contrary, should be rejected as unlikely, even though there was evidence which would favour them. The premises of science are subject to continuous modifications . . . Every established proposition of science enters into the current premises of science and affects the scientist's decision to accept an observation as a fact or to disregard it as probably unfounded. [The history of physics] refutes the widely-held view that scientists necessarily abandon a scientific proposition if a new observation conflicts with it . . . Stephen Toulmin has shown systematically that the framework of scientific theory contains general suppositions which cannot be put directly to an experimental test of truth or falsity.[25]

As Caudill points out, this pre-theoretical commitment among scientists to a framework or paradigm led Thomas Kuhn to speak of the "faith" aspect of science. Presuppositional frameworks guide the work of contemporary scientists. In Caudill's words, "to the extent that a set of unproved assumptions provides unity and guidance to a scientific discipline, one may speak of the religious or ideological character of science."[26] In this sense, evolutionary theory can present a religious perspective equal to that of creationism.

Caudill explains that the court's decision in this case was determined at the beginning by the presumption that creationism was religious and the presumption that evolution was not. The court emphasized the creationists' belief in supernatural intervention and their reliance on a spiritual, Biblical account of the history of the world. By contrast, the court characterized evolutionary science's emphasis on natural law as an empirical, falsifiable explanation. However, Caudill argues, creation scientists affirm natural laws, and they do empirical, falsifiable research. Moreover, both perspectives have foundational questions that they hope to verify. The court emphasized those of the creation scientist Biblical account but was unable to recognize the equally faith-based approach of evolution. In support of this position Caudill refers to Carl Sagan's television special "Cosmos." In this program scientists with an evolutionary outlook say that the "cosmos is all that is or ever will be," and it "is the universe that made us." The program is often shown in public schools where the students also learn that it is science that gives reliable knowledge, while religion is associated with narrowness of mind and bigotry.[27]

This identification of foundational beliefs as "religious" parallels the subjective, functionalist view of religion articulated in *Seeger*, but the court ignored it, failing even to address the issue. Moreover, the justices refused to consider the possibility that what to them was clearly a nonreligious, neutral teaching, to others *could* be a governmental establishment of religion. For the justices to dismiss this possibility as flying in the face of "common sense" illustrates an insensitivity to the difficulties inherent in First Amendment jurisprudence. However, it also illustrates another problem. Is *nonreligious* really the same as *neutral toward religion*?

All of these cases indicate that there are two major problems in articulating a definition of religion. First, in distinguishing the religious from the nonreligious those who most need protection, like Africa, might be left out because their views are not understood. Judges' own perspectives concerning religion may affect their decisions to the detriment of certain groups. In *Dade Schools* and *McLean* the court was dealing with a mainstream faith, Christianity, but believed that it knew better than the claimants what constituted the important elements of that faith.

Second, the courts continue to insist on the possibility of neutrality by the judiciary. But, the word neutrality means different things to different people—and, it means different things in different types of cases.

For example, in the free exercise cases that have come before the Supreme Court since *Seeger*, the emphasis has been on the tension between an admittedly religious practice and a competing regulatory interest of the state, such as the health or safety of citizens. Neutrality seems to mean treating foundational commitments equally. But, even if a court simply assumes an asserted religious practice to *be* religious, it still has to determine when governmental interests will override an individual's right to practice his or her religion. The problem is that a judge's approach to what religion is will affect his or her approach to when activity is to be protected.

In the establishment clause cases, on the other hand, neutrality seems to mean getting the religious out of the public sphere. Public schools may not teach courses from a religious or foundational, ultimate concern, point of view.

The next chapter examines the cases that develop each arm of religious freedom jurisprudence—free exercise and establishment clause. The point of this discussion is not to argue the wisdom of the judges' decisions, but rather to illustrate the connection between the definition of religion and the application of the constitutional tests that the judges have developed.

Notes

1. *Edwards v Aguillard*, 482 U.S. 578, 610 (1987). Portions of chapters one and two appeared in a different form in Julia Stronks, "The Courts' Definition of Religious Activity: Protection of Diversity or Imposition of a Majority View?" in Luis Lugo, *Religion, Public Life and the American Polity* (Knoxville: University of Tennessee Press, 1994), 145.

2. *Church of the Lukumi Babalu Aye v City of Hialeah, Florida*, 508 U.S. 520 (1993).

3. *Lukumi Babalu Aye,* 531.
4. *Lukumi Babalu Aye,* 536.
5. Stanley Ingber, "Religion or Ideology: A Needed Clarification of the Religion Clauses," *Stanford Law Review* 41 (1989): 233.
6. Douglas Laycock, "A Survey of Religious Liberty in the United States," *Ohio State Law Journal* 47 (1986): 409.
7. *Davis v Beason,* 133 U.S. 333 (1890).
8. *Torcaso v Watkins,* 367 U.S. 488, 495 (1961).
9. *United States v Seeger,* 380 U.S. 163 (1965).
10. *Seeger,* 168.
11. *Welsh v United States,* 398 U.S. 333, 339 (1970).
12. *Gillette v United States,* 401 U.S. 437 (1971).
13. *Malnak v Yogi,* 592 F.2d 197 (3rd Cir. 1979).
14. *Malnak,* 213.
15. *Malnak,* 213.
16. *Africa v Pennsylvania,* 622 F.2d 1025 (3rd Cir. 1981).
17. *Africa,* 1034.
18. Note, "Toward a Constitutional Definition of Religion," *Harvard Law Review* 91 (1978): 1056. This discussion of the *Africa* case draws from this law review Note.
19. *Africa,* 1061.
20. *Note,* "Toward a Constitutional Definition."
21. *Dettmer v. Landon,* 799 F.2d 929 (4th Cir.1986).
22. *Brown v Dade Christian School, Inc.,* 556 F.2d 310 (5th Cir. 1977).
23. *Brown,* 321.
24. *McLean v Arkansas Board of Education,* 529 F.Supp. 1255, 1274 (E D.Ark. 1982), emphasis added.
25. David Caudill, "Law and Worldview: Problems in the Creation-Science Controversy," *Journal of Law and Religion* 3 (1985): 11, 12.
26. Caudill, "Law and Worldview," 34.
27. Caudill, "Law and Worldview"; Richard Baer, "They Are Teaching Religion in the Public Schools," *Christianity Today* (Feb 17, 1984): 12.

Chapter Two

Guidance from the Supreme Court

This chapter illustrates the changes in the way the Supreme Court used its definition of religion to balance people's right to practice a religion against the government's interest in limiting their activity. The first section examines free exercise cases. The next section traces religion as it is used in establishment clause cases and demonstrates that part of our confusion about the nature of religion stems from our uncritical adoption of Thomas Jefferson's belief system.

Confusion in the Free Exercise Compelling Interest Standard

In 1878, a man named George Reynolds was convicted of polygamy. He defended his action as protected by the First Amendment, and this case is widely recognized as the beginning of free exercise jurisprudence.[1] As a Mormon, Reynolds argued that his act was based on a religious doctrine, and to convict him amounted to a violation of the free exercise clause. The Supreme Court, however, assumed that it was possible to separate religion and action. It concluded that even though polygamy may be based in religion, it was belief, not behavior, that was protected by the First Amendment. By prohibiting polygamy, Congress was protecting a "valid" societal interest.

The importance of this decision is twofold. First, it reveals the Court's understanding of religion as a matter of "private belief." As soon as a person acts on his or her belief in a way that does not conform to the will of the public, the public interest may control individuals' behavior by legally prohibiting it. Actions are under the authority of the government even if they are required by a belief system. Although the Court never questioned the "religiousness" of Mormonism, the assumption that private belief can be separated from public behavior reveals an approach to religion that can be traced through most of the Supreme Court cases.

Second, the Reynolds case is the first of a line of cases in which the Supreme Court has tried to determine the difference between religious activity in general and *protected* religious activity. It is the beginning of what Douglas Laycock has called "conscientious objector" law. Given the political process in this country, it often happens that "neutral" legislation, legislation that does not specify any particular religion, still has the effect of limiting people's expression of religion—prohibiting the sale or consumption of alcohol in the 1920s affected Catholic and other groups' participation in Communion; criminalizing drug use affects the Native American groups that ingest the cactus peyote in their sacraments; requiring autopsies affects groups that believe the body must be buried in a particular fashion after death; child labor laws affect children's participation in some groups' proselytizing requirements.

In certain cases, the state or federal legislators exercise sensitivity to religious groups and create exemptions from the law which accommodate the beliefs. Communion services were exempt from the Prohibition laws of the early twentieth century; some states exempt peyote use from illegal drug prosecutions. However, when the legislators refuse to accommodate religious beliefs, and individuals "conscientiously object" to the law, the courts step in to determine whether or not the state has the Constitutional obligation to exempt the religious objector from the law.

In making this decision the Supreme Court has fashioned a series of balancing tests. Today, whenever a state infringes on an individual's activity, the legislation is subject to one of the following tests: the rational relationship test (often referred to as a *reasonableness* standard), the strict scrutiny test (referred to as the *compelling interest* standard) or a test somewhere in between. If a right asserted by an individual is clearly protected in the Bill of Rights, such as free speech or equal protection, the Court subjects the legislation to strict scrutiny: is the state interest a *compelling interest*, and is the legislation the *least restrictive alternative* to achieve that interest. In other circumstances the Court defers to the legislators asking only if the legislation has a *legitimate* state interest and if the legislation is *rationally or reasonably related* to achieving the state's goal.

These tests may appear straightforward, but in theory and in practice their development has been fraught with confusion. Originally, the Court deferred to the legislature in free exercise challenges. Much later, the Court applied strict scrutiny, but only when the challenged regulation interfered directly with religious practices by criminalizing them. Then, the Court applied strict scrutiny to regulations that indirectly burdened religious practices when the activities were not criminalized but the statute made it more difficult or expensive for litigants to practice their religion. This increased the scope of free exercise protection. However, beginning in 1980 and culminating with the 1990 *Employment Divi-*

sion v Smith case, the Court has come full circle in its jurisprudence, returning to legislative deference.

In *Reynolds*, the polygamy case, the Court began its First Amendment analysis by balancing individual and state interests with one eye toward the will of the majority, not protection of minority rights.

> Congress was deprived of all legislative power over mere *opinion*, but was left free to reach *actions* which were in violation of social duties or subversive of good order.[2]

The test was deferential—judges looked only to their view or the majority's view of the good social order to determine whether or not legislation was "valid." The primary concern was that to do otherwise, to protect religious practices contrary to those recognized by the majority, would be to

> make professed doctrines of religious beliefs superior to the law of the land, and in effect to permit every citizen to become *a law unto himself*. Government could exist only in name under such circumstances.[3]

This language is important because it surfaces over and over as the Court applies its tests and as the tests change.

After *Reynolds*, the Court began to grapple with the nature of religion as it necessarily affects public life. In the 1892 case of *Church of the Holy Trinity v United States*, the Court had to balance a conflict between the free exercise of religion and a congressional statute prohibiting the importation of foreigners as laborers.[4] The Church wanted to hire a rector from Great Britain. This violated the law. In finding for the church, the Court recognized that while church and state may be separated, religion could not be separated from the people. In this case the Court acknowledged that religion is more than private belief; it may *of necessity* be related to business or employment practices.[5]

Then, in 1925 the Court ruled in favor of several private schools and against the state. In *Pierce v Society of Sisters*, Oregon required that all students attend public schools. When the law was challenged under the First Amendment, the Supreme Court said that although a state may require education, it may not force children into public schools.[6] The free exercise clause prohibits this violation of the rights of parents. Again, if religion comes to expression in the way parents choose schools then religion has an *unavoidable* impact in the public arena.[7] Religion is more than personal belief.

The test that the Court set forth in this case lays the groundwork for the reasonableness or rational relationship test articulated later. The Court said that

> rights guaranteed by the Constitution may not be abridged by legislation which has no *reasonable relation* to some purpose within the competency of the state. The fundamental theory of liberty upon

> which all governments in this Union repose excludes any general power of the state to standardize its children . . . . [The] injunctions here sought are not against the exercise of any proper power. Appellees asked protection against arbitrary, *unreasonable* and unlawful interference with their patrons and the consequent destruction of their business and property.[8]

In *Cantwell v Connecticut* the Court clearly articulated a balancing test with regard to First Amendment claims.[9] Cantwell, a Jehovah's Witness, was charged with violating a statute which prohibited the solicitation of money for religious ends without approval from the Secretary of Public Welfare. The Court said that because the state official was allowed to determine whether a cause was religious he was able to censor religion. The Court pointed out that the First Amendment involved both the freedom to believe and freedom to act. But, although the first concept was absolute, the second was protected only under certain circumstances. Freedom to act was subject to a two-part test: does the government action in question limit religious belief or activity, and if so, is the government action *necessary* to protect the peace, good order and comfort of the community. The assumption in *Reynolds*, that the will of the majority created a valid state interest, is no longer sufficient. Although the public order and comfort of the community as a whole still takes precedence over the individual's expression of religion, the test requires that the legislation be necessary, not just desirable, for the protection of the community.

In 1963, the Court appeared to reject the distinction between private belief and action, and it changed the test once more, employing the "strict scrutiny standard." In *Sherbert v Verner* the plaintiff was a Seventh-Day Adventist working a five-day week in a textile mill.[10] However, when the mill changed its schedule to a six-day workweek which conflicted with her worship on Saturdays, Sherbert refused to work on Saturdays and was fired. When she applied for unemployment compensation, she was denied benefits. The Supreme Court ruled that Sherbert was entitled to unemployment compensation since her right to the free exercise of her religion could not be infringed by the government agency. It was true that the government agency had not tried to criminalize her religious expression, but when government policy made her religious expression more difficult it violated the free exercise clause.

In *Sherbert*, Justice Brennan's analysis specifically shifted the burden of proof from the religious objector to the state: after an initial showing by the objector that a religious interest was impaired, the state must assert a compelling government interest and show that there was no less restrictive means to further this interest.

> It is basic that no showing *merely of a rational relationship* to some colorable state interest would suffice; in this highly sensitive constitutional area only the gravest abuses, endangering paramount interest, give occasion for permissible limitation.[11]

The state asserted as its interest the fact that to allow a claim to receive unemployment insurance under these circumstances would give rise to an unmanageable number of lawless people fraudulently claiming that they quit their jobs because of religious reasons. This concern parallels the Court's concern in *Reynolds*, that to allow one exemption would permit citizens to become laws unto themselves. While this possibility was determinative in *Reynolds*, it failed in *Sherbert*. The Supreme Court easily dismissed the state's concern by saying that there was no specific evidence that this lawlessness would happen.

The compelling interest test was developed further in *Wisconsin v Yoder*.[12] In this case the Amish fought the Wisconsin law requiring school attendance for all children. In holding that the regulation burdened the free exercise of religion, the Court carefully examined the interests of both the Amish and the state. It analyzed the arguments set forth by each side, and it articulated the strengths and weaknesses of each. The Court concluded that the state's interest in preparing children to be independent in the world could be met with alternatives other than compulsory education by state certified schools. Thus, the "less restrictive alternative" arm of the strict scrutiny test was not met.

But, although the interests of the Amish were protected in this case, *Yoder* illustrates the significance of the definitional issue. Chief Justice Burger did seem to eliminate the belief/action dichotomy. He said that the failure of Amish parents to send their children to public high school was not just illegal public "action" subject to the criminal law. The action was an expression of faith. In this case "belief and action cannot be neatly confined in logic-tight compartments."[13] However, Burger also said that the Amish could be protected only because they adhered to a truly "religious" belief.

> A way of life, however virtuous and admirable, may not be interposed as a barrier to reasonable state regulation of education if it is based on purely secular considerations; to have the protection of the Religion Clauses, the claims must be rooted in religious belief.[14]

In one analysis of Burger's decision, historian Rockne McCarthy argues that Burger's assumptions reveal his preconception about religion, and they lead to confusion about the purpose and the breadth of protection that the First Amendment entails. First, Burger believes it is possible to distinguish those people whose lives are determined by religion from those who are guided by secular considerations. The weakness of this assumption is illustrated by the cases in which federal courts have tried to make the distinction. Religion cannot be clearly distinguished from secularity or irreligion.

McCarthy explains that Burger also assumes that the First Amendment defines religion in a way that is sufficient to keep it from protecting irreligious or nonreligious persons. And, says McCarthy, Burger is convinced that it is legitimate for only these irreligious people to be subject to the majoritarian educational requirements that are imposed on citizens. As in the cases of military conscientious objectors and *Africa*, those people who assert a worldview that is a "moral code" rather than a "religion" do not escape the requirement of the law.

Burger said that the concept of ordered liberty requires a distinction between moral and religious belief. Liberty

> precludes allowing every person to make his own standards on matters of conduct in which society as a whole has important interests. Thus, if the Amish asserted their claims because of their subjective evaluation and rejection of the contemporary secular values accepted by the majority, much as Thoreau rejected the social values of his time and isolated himself at Walden Pond, their claims would not rest on a religious basis. Thoreau's choice was *philosophical and personal rather than religious*, and such belief does not rise to the demands of the Religion Clauses.[15]

When Burger says that the "secular values of the majority" have moral authority over "society as a whole" he expresses his own philosophy. Only if people can appeal to the religion clauses with a *private* religion may they be exempt from the rules of the majority.[16] What Burger does not do is to demonstrate why the Amish way of life is religious while others are not religious. McCarthy asks, why are Thoreau's beliefs nonreligious when, in fact, Thoreau may well have believed that his life was a religious commitment?

Over the next ten years the Court continued to protect religious interests, but was not able to clear up the confusion about religious versus moral or philosophical beliefs. In the following two cases lower courts had sustained government action, arguing that the claimant's objection to the regulation was *philosophical* rather than religious. The Supreme Court overruled.

In *Wooley v Maynard* a New Hampshire statute required that all passenger vehicle license plates display the state motto "Live Free or Die."[17] The petitioner, a Jehovah's Witness, covered the motto on this license plate, claiming that its message was repugnant to his moral, religious and political beliefs. The state alleged that the display of the motto served to facilitate the differentiation of passenger vehicles from other types of vehicles and promoted an appreciation of history, state pride and individualism. The Court did not address whether the motto was truly antithetical to the Jehovah's Witness religion, nor did it determine whether a state-promoted individualism was "neutral" with regard to other religions. Rather, using the strict scrutiny test, the Court simply asserted that the state interest was not compelling enough, nor was the least restrictive alternative used to achieve the state interest.

In the 1981 case *Thomas v Indiana Employment Security Division,* the Supreme Court, citing *Yoder* and *Sherbert*, reversed a lower court ruling that denied a Jehovah's Witness unemployment compensation when he was fired for refusing work for religious reasons.[18] Thomas had objected to a transfer within his steel processing plant that would have involved him more directly in the production of munitions. Other Jehovah's Witnesses did work in the plant and this led the lower court to determine that it was Thomas's personal philosophy, not religion, that kept him from his work. The Supreme Court rejected the lower court's determination that Thomas had made a personal philosophical choice rather than a religious one.

> Although the claimant's reasons for quitting were described as religious, it was unclear what his belief was, and what the religious basis of his belief was. In [the lower] court's view, Thomas had made a merely "*personal philosophical choice rather than a religious choice.*"[19]

As in *Sherbert*, even though Thomas's religious activity was not criminalized by the government activity, the government made his religious expression more difficult with its policy. This violated the First Amendment.

Unfortunately, although the Court did protect Thomas's religious expression it still failed to show how religious claims ought to be examined. Even though Thomas's religion was recognized by the Court, the opinion stated

> intrafaith differences of [this] kind are not uncommon among followers of a particular creed, and the judicial process is singularly ill equipped to resolve such differences in relation to the Religion Clauses. *One can, of course, imagine an asserted claim so bizarre, so clearly nonreligious* in motivation, as not to be entitled to protection under the Free Exercise Clause.[20]

However, as *Africa* illustrates, what is bizarre to a court may well be religious to a litigant.

The dissent in *Thomas* was written by William Rehnquist who is today the Chief Justice of the Supreme Court. The dissent is important because Rehnquist's concerns foreshadow a major change in First Amendment protection. He says,

> [w]here, as here, a State has enacted a general statute, the purpose and effect of which is to advance the State's secular goals, the Free Exercise Clause does not in my view require the State to conform that statute to the dictates of religious conscience of any group.[21]

Rehnquist's assumption is that government interests are obviously different from religious interests in that they are "secular." But, he makes this statement without clearly articulating what he means by religion. Although Rehnquist claims that he is moving the Court away from the problems experienced when it tries to define religion, his own assumption reflects a particular cultural bias about the ability of a government to be truly neutral toward "religious" interests. He further confuses the issue by stating in a footnote that this case is distinguishable from *Sherbert* because Thomas left his job for purely personal reasons, whereas Sherbert left for religious reasons.

In addition, Rehnquist's willingness to defer to legislatures in determining when religion should be protected calls up the analysis of the 1878 *Reynolds* case. Rehnquist's reliance on *Reynolds* is even more evident when he expresses his fear:

> The [Court] . . . suggests that a person who leaves his job for purely "personal philosophical choices" will be constitutionally entitled to unemployment benefits. If that is true, the implications of today's decision are enormous. Persons will then be able to quit their jobs, assert they did so for personal reasons, and collect unemployment insurance. We could surely expect the State's limited funds allotted for unemployment insurance to be quickly depleted. [22]

This is the same fear the *Reynolds* court expressed when it said exceptions to the law brought lawlessness, and it is the same fear that the *Sherbert* court rejected saying no evidence supported this type of concern.

Beginning in the 1980s the Supreme Court developed Rehnquist's dissent in *Thomas* and began to deny claims by religious objectors seeking relief from regulations that appeared to be neutral but, in fact, limited their religious expression. In *United States v Lee* the Court rejected an Amish farmer's request to be exempt from social security taxes.[23] The Court acknowledged the sincerity of Lee's religious objection to mandatory social security payments, but said that the government interest in collecting taxes was compelling. The Court did not explain why the federal interest in collecting taxes was more compelling than a state interest in educating children (*Yoder*) or the federal interest in regulating unemployment (*Sherbert* and *Thomas*). This case and those following can be explained by a change in the political persuasion of the Court, but they also indicate that the Supreme Court's approach to religious protection is both flexible and confused. The various tests and the varied ways in which they are applied allow the Court to justify any result it wishes. Moreover, they illustrate the Court's inability to develop a comprehensive theory about religious protection, an inability that stems in part from the confusion about what religion is and what it is not.

In *Bowen v Roy* the Court faced a free exercise challenge brought on behalf of a Native American child.[24] The argument was that statutory requirements conditioning welfare benefits on parents' willingness to use the Social Security number of their child violated the family's religious freedom. The parents' objection was that the use of the number would rob the child of her spirit. A plurality of the Court denied Roy's claim. The judges distinguished between those claims that involved the mere denial of a government benefit and those that imposed criminal sanctions on conduct that had religious implications. This distinction was what *Sherbert* and *Thomas*, both government benefits cases, had denied.

Another significant aspect of this case is that three concurring members of the Court advocated a lower standard of review than the strict scrutiny test. Applying this lower standard, these three determined that the Social Security number requirement was a "reasonable" means of promoting the "legitimate" public interest to prevent proliferation of fraud. Because a lower test was used, this interest outweighed the parents' free exercise interest. The previous cases which claimed clear evidence had to exist that fraud actually would occur were not controlling because they were determined with a more strict test. Although a decision by three members of the Court does not by itself change precedent, the case lay the groundwork for future decisions.

During the same period that *Lee* and *Roy* were decided, the Court decided three free exercise cases in which the majority of the justices applied the lower "reasonableness" test rather than the strict scrutiny test. In each case the Court articulated a reason why the particular facts warranted an exception to the strict scrutiny standard, but by 1990 it became clear that these cases were the beginning of a new First Amendment era. In *Goldman v Weinberger* the Court upheld an Air Force regulation prohibiting indoor headgear.[25] Goldman, a captain in the Air Force, wore a yarmulke. When he refused to remove it during a court proceeding, he was told that it violated military regulations. He sued claiming infringement of First Amendment rights. In analyzing the case, the Supreme Court declined to apply the standard of strict scrutiny developed in *Sherbert*, requiring only that the regulation advance "legitimate" military ends.

Justice Rehnquist wrote the Court's opinion and, given his dissent in *Thomas*, it is not surprising that the Court subjected the military interest to no examination at all. The Court specifically rejected Goldman's argument that the military should justify its concern that allowing an exemption to the regulation would affect discipline. Rather, citing the importance of deference to the professional judgment of military authorities, the Court accepted without discussion the military's justification for its regulation—the need for uniformity in the military.

A second exception to the rule of strict scrutiny was set forth in *Lyng v Northwest Indian Cemetery Protection Assn.*[26] In this case Native Americans objected to the government's plan to build a highway on government land that ran through sacred ground. The ground was used by the group in religious ceremonies, and the road would preclude the worship because no other land had the same religious significance. The Court held that government was not barred from constructing a road. It stated that the Free Exercise Clause does not give individuals the right to dictate to the government how to conduct its internal affairs or how to use its own land. The government was not required to show a compelling justification for its actions when the burden on a claimant was simply the "incidental effect" of a government program. In the Court's opinion the government's program may have rendered the religious activity more difficult, but it did not force the Native Americans to act in ways contrary to their beliefs. In this case the Court covertly concluded that it knew better than the Native Americans which elements of the faith were significant and which were incidental. The fact that Indian ceremony relates to land made sacred for specific reasons was not recognized.

In the third case the free exercise rights of prisoners were addressed.[27] Muslim prisoners' worship at Friday prayer services was denied because prison regulations required those who worked outside the prison to return at specific hours. The Court held that because of the special situation of prisons, the regulations which burdened Constitutional rights would from now on be judged by a "reasonableness" test rather than the strict scrutiny test.

Although there may be legitimate reasons for prison officials to limit religious expression by inmates, the Court's deference to administrative decisions, its refusal to question legislative authority and its willingness to lower the balancing test in all three of these cases is significant because it foreshadows an important change in religious freedom jurisprudence.

In 1990 when the Supreme Court handed down *Employment Division v Smith*, Constitutional scholars across the nation decried the case as a disaster in First Amendment jurisprudence.[28] Justice Scalia wrote the opinion which held that the right of free exercise does not relieve an individual of the obligation to comply with a valid and neutral law of general applicability just because he or she thinks the law constricts activity that a religion requires.

In *Smith* two Native American men claimed that an EEOC decision denying their plea for unemployment insurance discriminated against them on the basis of their religion. The EEOC denied the claim because the men were fired from their jobs for ingesting peyote, a hallucinogenic cactus, during religious ceremonies. The men were fired from their jobs for participating in wrongful conduct. This precluded them from collecting unemployment insurance.

The facts and result in *Smith* are relatively insignificant in terms of free exercise claims. Over the years in cases like *Roy* many litigants have been denied governmental benefits because the state interest was compelling and outweighed their right to religious expression. The importance of *Smith* lies in the Court's specific rejection of the compelling interest test. A plurality of the Court, four justices, said that an individual's religious beliefs do not excuse him from compliance with an otherwise "valid" law. In determining whether or not the legislation was "valid" the Court asked if it was "reasonable."

Furthermore, the Court acknowledged that leaving accommodation of religious expression to the legislative political process could place minority religions at a disadvantage. Calling this the "unavoidable consequence of democratic government," the Court stated that it was preferred to a system in which each conscience is a law unto itself. Note the similarity of this case to *Reynolds*, the 1878 polygamy case. A state statute must be "valid," and it is assumed that when the majority agrees on a statute, validity occurs. And, the primary reason for refusing exemption for those claimants who say the law violates their religious freedom is that to do otherwise would bring on a lawless society. In the span of 120 years, the Supreme Court has come full circle in applying its First Amendment test. Beliefs are protected but not actions.

Definition of Religion in Establishment Clause Cases

Supreme Court discussion of the establishment clause of the First Amendment begins with an analysis of the *Everson* case of 1947. In this case, New Jersey parents received local tax grants to reimburse them for the bus trips of their children to Catholic schools. By a 5-4 decision, the justices determined that tax supported bus rides to sectarian Catholic schools were "secular." Justice Black, in delivering the opinion of the Court said:

> The "establishment of religion" clause of the First Amendment means at least this: Neither a state nor the Federal Government can set up a church. Neither can it pass laws which aid one religion, aid all religions, or prefer one religion over another. Neither can it force nor influence a person to go to or remain away from church against his will or force him to profess a belief or disbelief in any religion. No person can be punished for entertaining or professing religious beliefs or disbeliefs, for church attendance or non-attendance. In the words of Jefferson, the clause against establishment of religion by law was intended to erect a "wall of separation between Church and State."[29]

Rockne McCarthy points out that this decision assumed the legitimacy of interpreting the First Amendment in Jeffersonian terms. Black articulated the standard of "separation of church and state" which stems from the general propositions of Jefferson. Since the state should do nothing to aid sectarian religion, it should be prohibited from giving any aid to nonpublic, religious institutions, including schools. However, the Court did allow New Jersey to reimburse *parents* of nonpublic school children for the costs of busing their children to school. The Court said that because the aid had a neutral public purpose which was to benefit children, the aid itself was not religious even though the children's *education* was religious.

The merit of this argument depends on the acceptance of a religious/secular dichotomy. To Justice Black, neutrality occurred when parents and children could receive support for secular activities like education. What the parents did with the support was up to them. If they acted on their private religious beliefs in spending the aid, that was fine. But, not everyone accepted this dichotomy, and not everyone agreed with Justice Black's jurisprudence. Several years later, a new "neutrality" standard was proposed.

In 1963 *Schempp v District of Abington* focused on the use of Bible reading and recitation of the Lord's Prayer as part of the opening exercises in a public school.[30] In declaring the use of the Bible and prayer to be unconstitutional, the Court said "They are religious exercises, required by the state in violation of the command of the First Amendment that the Government maintain *strict neutrality*, neither aiding nor opposing religion."[31] According to this principle, the government must be neutral in religious matters. The definition of neutrality was as follows: If the advancement or inhibition of religion is the primary legislative purpose or effect of a law, it violates the establishment clause because it is not neutral. This test was developed further a few years later on.[32] In *Lemon*, the Court ruled as unconstitutional a government-funding project that allowed the teaching of "secular" courses in private elementary and secondary schools. The significance of *Lemon* is that it articulated a test for determining when a government action established religion:

- The action must have a secular legislative purpose—did legislators have a nonreligious, secular purpose in mind or were they motivated by religious, sectarian goals?
- The action's principal or primary effect must be one that neither advances nor inhibits religion: does it have a secular effect; is it neutral in regard to religion, neither helping nor hindering it?
- The action must not foster an excessive government entanglement with religion—entanglement is often administrative: does the statute involve a continuing relationship between the church and government?

But, the test assumes a common understanding of what it means to be secular and what it means to be religious. The very same year that *Lemon* said government cannot fund secular subjects at faith-based schools, *Tilton* held that government could fund buildings at faith-based universities.[33] Colleges could receive government aid but aid was restricted at lower levels. Justice Burger's reconciliation of these cases hinged on his finding that in the *Tilton* case the aid was for buildings and services which were religiously "neutral whereas in the *Lemon* case the aid subsidized teachers, who are not necessarily religiously neutral."[34] He acknowledged the difficulty of this distinction when he said "the line of separation between church and state, far from being a 'wall,' is a blurred, indistinct and variable barrier depending on all the circumstances of a particular relationship."[35] Burger's acknowledgment is critical because he sets the Supreme Court up for years of discussion about the nature of religion. Much of the discussion about religious activity, in turn, hinges on whether religion is private or public.

There are two classic analyses that inform most First Amendment jurisprudence: the "separationist" perspective, which is also called "strict separationism" or "strict neutrality," and the "accommodationist" perspective, which includes "non-preferentialism" and a variety of other "neutrality" variations. In general, each of the theories selects one of the religion clauses and elevates it to a priority higher than the other. Separationists stress the establishment clause; accommodationists stress the free exercise clause.

Although religious freedom seems to call for accommodation of religion, the separation principle imbedded in the establishment clause holds this governmental accommodation to be suspect. The tension stems from the fact that the

> principle of religious liberty has an expanding dynamic built into it, calling for a positive and active legal attitude towards claims to have one's religious requirements respected through legal accommodation, exemption, privileges, subsidies. This very dynamic threatens to undermine the disengagement of the state from religious matters demanded by the principle of separation.[36]

The tension is further exacerbated by the fact that the clauses seem to contradict each other. Deference to free exercise leads to government protection of religion which can be construed as establishment. Justice Sandra Day O'Connor realized this when she observed the following.

> On the one hand, a rigid application of the *Lemon* test would invalidate legislation exempting religious observers from generally applicable government obligations. By definition, such legislation has a religious purpose and effect in promoting the free exercise of religion. On the other hand, judicial deference to all legislation that purports to facilitate the free exercise of religion would completely vitiate the Establishment Clause. Any statute pertaining to religion can be viewed as an "accommodation" of free exercise rights.[37]

Some scholars have asserted that the cause for the tension is inherent in the reading of the First Amendment, even that it is an acceptable way to balance citizens' rights. Others argue that the confusion stems from the piecemeal way in which the clauses were incorporated into the Fourteenth Amendment. However, most work critical of religious freedom jurisprudence simply assumes that the tension would disappear if only judges would adhere to the correct legal theory or constitutional interpretation.

Separationists

Separationists argue that most forms of government support for religion are prohibited by the establishment clause and its principle of strict separation of church and state. They invoke the Jeffersonian metaphor "wall of separation" to illustrate their understanding of the appropriate relationship between the church and the state. Some argue that the establishment clause forbids Congress to provide any form of legitimization or economic assistance to religious or religiously affiliated organizations. They say that expression of faith is allowed, but it is private and ought not to involve public funds or public support. Others argue that separation means the government must maintain a "hands off" approach to religious institutions. Again, faith is private, and in order to practice their faith, people must be free from government scrutiny.

Although separationism is a very popular American concept, the phrase is not in the Constitution and the judges that apply separationism to their cases face two significant problems. First, even if you believe that faith is private and should be kept out of the public arena, the fact is that issues relating to religious expression *unavoidably* involve the public domain. Rearing and schooling of children involves family and education law; eating and drinking in sacraments involves the Food and Drug Administration; hiring and firing of employees involves U.S. labor law. Second, historically there has been both enormous financial support of religious institutions, and support in all three government branches for public acknowledgment of religion. Churches receive tax breaks even while they benefit from the government services (fire department, police protection) that are supposed to be paid for by those taxes. Christian universities receive federal support. In the book *Private Churches and Public Money* Paul Weber documents hundreds of ways in which religious institutions benefit financially from the government.[38] Faith, government and religious institutions *are* intertwined—the important thing is to figure out how the law should define their *legal* parameters.

Accommodationism

Accommodationists or nonpreferentialists argue that government support for religion is required by the free exercise clause and its principle of state accommodation of religion and the church. They believe that the establishment clause is subordinate to the free exercise clause. Government must not just allow people to practice their faiths, but government has a specific duty to accommodate religious belief. This occurs through financial assistance and through exemptions to the laws that require people to act in ways contrary to their religious faiths. Accommodationists argue that the establishment clause was designed to prohibit discrimination *between* religions.

The accommodationist approach, however, leaves completely unresolved how "religion" or "religious activity" is to be defined. Accommodationists may argue for a very broad protection of religion, but they do not press themselves on the definitional issue. For example, what is a religious institution? Is there a difference between a church that wants to hire only Christians and a Christian business that will not hire Jews? What about a white supremacist political organization that will not hire blacks? Is there a difference between and among conscientious objectors who will not go to war because they are pacifists, because they just do not like war, because they are morally opposed to war, or because they believe in the just war theory and this particular war does not fit in? Why does "religion" get special treatment but political philosophy or feminist approaches to life do not? The idea that only religious belief gets protection leads into a tangled thicket when accommodationists have to explain why one belief is religious and another is not.

Over the history of religious freedom jurisprudence, the Supreme Court decisions have reflected both the separationist and the accommodationist perspectives. John Witte, a legal scholar at Emory University law school, suggests that the persistence of this separatist/accommodationist dialectic is not accidental, but that the dialectic is inherent in the religion clauses themselves. The religion clauses are the product of both enlightenment politics and evangelical theology. He argues that they reflect the concerns of enlightenment politicians to protect politics and the state from the intrusions of religion and the church. They also reflect the desire of evangelical theologians to protect religion and the church from the intrusions of politics and the state. The clauses are a result of the give and take of a pluralistic democracy. Competing or conflicting values are to be expected, given the compromises that were necessary at the time.

Law professor MaryAnn Glendon, however, suggests that much of the tension is not inherent in the clauses, but was caused by the history of the incorporation of the clauses.[39] The free exercise clause was addressed and incorporated onto the states by the Supreme Court prior to the 1940s. In its interpretation of the clause in *Cantwell* the Court began the development of what became the compelling interest test.

In early cases, the Court employed a balancing approach that weighed the infringement on an individual's interests in being free of state interference, against the burden that an exemption would place on the state's regulatory interests. The definition of religion in these cases was not critical. The emphasis was on the balance. Glendon explains that the cases never examined the effect of *both* clauses on activity, so the nature of the establishment of religion was not considered.

But, because the Court had, at this point, spent many years acting as if free exercise and establishment were not related, "the Court became susceptible to the argument that the establishment provision represented its own independent set of values."[40] When the question of the incorporation of the establishment provision reached the Court in the 1947 *Everson* case, "the stage was set for the Justices to adopt a controversial and ahistorical interpretation of that language."[41]

In *Everson*, the Court accepted one particular view of the essential purpose of the Constitution's religion language. In doing so, the Court adopted a perspective that had been articulated by Justice Felix Frankfurter in earlier dissents. In 1943, Justice Frankfurter dissented when the Court found that a state may not tax the sale of religious literature by Jehovah's Witnesses.[42] Frankfurter tax the sale of religious literature by Jehovah's Witnesses.[42] Frankfurter claimed that to exempt the proselytizers from taxation offended "the most important of all aspects of religious freedom in this country, namely that of the separation of church and state."[43] Therefore, the free exercise clause should fail in the face of "separationism." Glendon explains that though the Court had thus far *never* allowed separationism to govern its interpretation of the free exercise clause, it did make separationism central to its establishment interpretation.

Glendon argues that by accepting Frankfurter's language, the Court inappropriately elevated the separation of church and state to the status of a constitutional end in itself. This

> historic move was as unreflective as it was fateful. The various opinion writers in *Everson* seemed unaware of the free exercise implications of their acceptance of separation as an independent constitutional value.[44]

By setting the interpretation of establishment on a "different course" from that of free exercise, says Glendon, the Justices *created* an appearance of conflict between two provisions that "history and text suggest were meant to work together in the service of religious liberty."[45] The case was so important because in it the Court adopted phrases like "the *most important of all* aspects of religious freedom in this country, [is] that of the separation of church and state."[46] But it was also important because it demonstrates the struggle that judges were beginning to have about the relationship of religion to the rest of life.

Remember that in *Everson* the Court had to determine whether the First Amendment allowed New Jersey to use taxpayer money to pay for the transportation by public bus of children to church-run schools. Justice Black's majority opinion claimed that all government laws or expenditures that aid religion *in any way* are invalid, but, at the same time, he admitted that this assertion could not be taken literally. So, despite his claims that separationism had to define jurisprudence, he allowed the reimbursements to the parents of sectarian school children.

The dissenters argued that the "undertones of the opinion, advocating complete and uncompromising separation of Church from State, seem utterly discordant with its conclusion yielding support to their commingling in educational matters."[47] Further, Justice Rutledge claimed that the purpose of the First Amendment was "to create a *complete and permanent separation* of the spheres of religious activity and civil authority by comprehensively forbidding every form of public aid or support for religion."[48] Glendon observes that Rutledge's opinion

> affords an instructive glimpse of an influential assumption at the heart of much separationist thinking about the establishment language: the assumption that *religion is or ought to be a wholly*

> *"private" matter*. Rutledge took it as self-evident that "the realm of religious training and belief remains, as the Amendment made it, *the kingdom of the individual man and his God,*" and that "it should be kept *inviolably private*." This theme was to recur frequently in church-state opinions over the years. For many Justices, the only constitutionally cognizable religious experiences were those that implicated the solitary individual. A subtheme was that religious experience is separable from the rest of human life and activity.[49]

The problem that the judges were to face as they decided more and more cases is illustrated by the discussion in *Everson*. Separation is desired by the judges, but the fact is, religion has an unavoidable impact on public life. As Black admitted, complete separation was not possible, so how should the balance be made?

For the following fifty years, the judges went back and forth. Separationism dominated in the 1940s. Then, a language of nonhostility, or "neutrality" developed. In *Everson*, Black had commented that despite the need for separation, government did not have to be hostile to religion. Later cases picked up on this language, arguing that religion could even be accommodated.

Over the past decades, the Court has struck down government policies that directly supported religious ritual like prayer in schools, but prayer and chaplains in legislative sessions were upheld. Direct public assistance to sectarian schools was struck down, but public assistance to sectarian social service agencies was accepted. Despite its separation language, the Court has upheld state laws that required stores to close on the Sabbath despite the appearance of support to Christians at the expense of Jews, and despite the appearance of establishment of religion at the expense of nonreligious belief. Government holiday displays of Christian artifacts have been denied, but some displays of Jewish artifacts have been accepted. Tax exemptions for religious institutions have also been upheld. In all of these cases, separationist language competed with accommodationist language. The Jeffersonian "wall" metaphor was held up against the willingness of the Framers to emphasize religious protections to the extent that they dedicated two clauses of an amendment to it.

Jefferson, the Constitution and Religion

The history of the church in early America sheds light on the assumptions that frame judicial reasoning today. In pre-Revolutionary Virginia, the Church of England was established as the state's formal religion. Support for the church was mandatory, and adherents to other traditions were often punished.

After the American Revolution, however, Virginian politicians were involved in reconsideration of church/state relations. Scholars tell us that three groups defined this debate over religious freedom: the traditionalists, the enlightenment rationalists and the evangelical pietists. The traditionalists believed that good government could occur only through formal establishment of a religion by the state.

The pietists stood in the tradition of Roger Williams, who called for a wall of separation between the garden of the church and the wilderness of the world. He argued that involving the government in church affairs would hurt the institution of the church and religious belief itself.

The third group, the rationalists, included Madison and Jefferson. Madison's argument for separation of church and state is set forth in his "Memorial and Remonstrance" written against the passage of an Assessment Bill which was designed to use state funds to support Christian teachers. The Memorial stated that no one should be taxed to support any sort of religious activity nor should citizenship in any way be impaired because of religious views. Madison argued that religion was a private matter, and he argued with the pietists for a separation of church and state.

Jefferson furthered Madison's perspective. He was responsible for drafting the "Bill for Establishing Religious Freedom." He agreed with Madison that religion was a personal matter, and he argued that the morals necessary for the maintenance of a good society were determined by reason not religion. In Jefferson's letter to the Danbury Baptist Association in 1802, Jefferson articulated his conviction that separation of church and state was essential. It is in this letter that the phrase "wall of separation" between church and state first appears.

> Believing with you that religion is a matter which lies solely between man and his God, that he owes account to none other for his faith or his worship, that the legislative power of government reach actions only, and not opinions, I contemplate with sovereign reverence that this legislature should "make no law respecting an establishment of religion, or prohibiting the free exercise thereof," thus building a wall of separation between church and state.[50]

In 1779, Jefferson's bill for religious liberty had been ignored by the Virginia legislature. In 1785, however, Madison reintroduced Jefferson's bill, and it passed in the House by a majority of 74-20. Many people attribute this switch to the number of supportive letters sent by various pietists to the legislature that year.[51] Despite their different views of life, the rationalists and pietists both had an interest in the disestablishment of the Church of England.

The interesting thing for the definition of religion, however, was that the pietists accepted Jeffersonian and Madisonian argument that private faith was not a public matter. If Christianity was really a private matter, it would not be allowed to direct the way in which public policy would be articulated. The foundation for policy had to come from somewhere else. It is here that Thomas Jefferson's philosophy impacts our current debate about the nature of religious belief. Historians like Rockne McCarthy, William Harper, James Skillen, Richard Baer, Thomas Buckley and others demonstrate that Jefferson's work with the pietists had a profound political impact. By encouraging pietists to keep their organized religions in the private, personal domain, Jefferson was able to define a political order based on his own personal philosophy and commitment to rationalism. This order was not considered to be religious because it was public, and not private. However, this order did provide a particular view of life and man's responsibility in that life.

Jefferson argued that morality was determined by reason, and he believed that all people, no matter what their private religion, had this same common morality. Nature's God gave common sense to all, and this common sense could be counted on to provide consensus about what the public order should look like. As long as "sectarians" kept their beliefs out of the public order, everything was fine. Freedom of religion meant that they could believe what they wanted, but the public order would be defined only by that morality on which all could, with their common sense, agree. In a letter to James Fishback written in 1809 Jefferson makes the following statement:

> the interests of society require the observation of those moral precepts only in which all religions agree . . . we should not intermeddle with the particular dogmas in which all religions differ, and which are totally unconnected with morality . . . The practice of morality being necessary for the well-being of society, he [God] has taken care to impress its precepts so indelibly on our hearts that they shall not be effaced by the subtleties of our brain.[52]

The churches were engaged in a battle about establishment of religion, and they knew they were losing the battle. They were also fighting among themselves about the nature of truth, and they were all afraid of having any one denomination able to use the government to force a perspective on truth. It became clear that it was to their benefit to accept a Jeffersonian approach to the public order as long as they would be left alone in their private, ecclesiastical world without interference from government. Eventually, many people came to believe that God involved the private and the personal, while the public, political area did not involve God.

Now, was Jefferson's moral order as religious as was the pietists? It depends on what you mean by religion. If you take a *Davis* approach to religion, the answer is probably *no*. However, if you take a *Seeger* approach to religion as an ultimate value system, the answer is probably *yes*.

The problem was that the churches, including the pietists, did not understand that Jefferson's moral philosophy could act as a religion in the broad sense. Then, because Jefferson's perspective was not called a religion, separation of church and state came to mean church faith is private, but morality of the public order, based on a vision of common sense, was not faith.

McCarthy and others explain that by the end of the nineteenth century, the United States had generally accepted Jefferson's version of the separation of church and state. This acceptance included a consensus that religion was related to churches and to personal, private faith. Religious freedom was freedom of "personal conviction" and freedom of "ecclesiastical association."[53] Churches and private beliefs were not to be limited or encouraged by government; the government was "neutral" toward religion. The role of the government was to serve the "secular interest" as defined by a neutral, majoritarian consensus.

Is it this public/private split, the idea that what is public is "nonreligious" or neutral, that is at the foundation of American courts' confusion in addressing the question "what is religion?" There are some significant problems with the assumption that religion is merely private.

One problem is that when we talk casually about separation of church and state, we can easily miss the ways in which the state and other public entities reflect a particular religious outlook. Government institutions offer public acknowledgment of the importance of religion in presidential inaugurations and speeches, courtroom proceedings and legislative sessions. Prayers, blessings or oaths invoking God's name are common to each branch of government. This, along with the belief that what is "religious" is private but what is public may be controlled by the majority, has led some to conclude that a "religiosity," a civil religion, defines the nation's public life. Civil religion is a "shared public statement of beliefs and symbols" which indicate an "accepted religious legitimation of political authority."[54] In the words of historian Sidney Mead, American culture exhibits

> the religion of the democratic society and nation. This was rooted in the rationalism of the Enlightenment . . . and was articulated in terms of the destiny of America, under God, to be fulfilled by perfecting the democratic way of life for the example and betterment of all mankind.[55]

This civil religion results in unexamined societal assumptions about legitimate state interests or appropriate behavior of individuals. It is a "cultural bias" which undermines equal treatment of the religious and the nonreligious. Judges come to their cases as part of this cultural or majoritarian consensus—this is evident in their approach to what is and what is not religious activity.

A second problem is that judicial beliefs that religion can be and must be excluded from the public sphere ignore the all-encompassing nature of religion. Many faiths articulate a worldview in which the religion has a necessary impact on the public arena—including schooling of children, employment decisions, and the use of money such as tax funds. This approach highlights the relationship between the free exercise clause and the establishment clause in that sometimes when people are prohibited by government from exercising their religion they are coerced into participating in what they view as an established government religion. For example, when an employer believes that his religion prohibits him from hiring people from outside his or her faith, the government's insistence on non-discrimination *becomes* a religious statement for that employer. The government's position also reflects a fundamental belief sanctioned by majoritarian consensus. Critics of this argument will say that government endorsement of nondiscrimination in employment is "neutral" toward religion, but if a person believes that all of life is religious, can the government endorsement really be neutral?

Scholars have attributed the confusion that dominates religious freedom jurisprudence to a tension in the clauses of the First Amendment, or to incorrect constitutional adjudication. But, is it really a tension between the clauses or could the problem be related to our vision of what "religion" really is? If you examine the cases carefully, the issue of definitions becomes critical. The next chapters demonstrate this problem.

Notes

1. *Reynolds v United States,* 98 U.S. 145 (1878).
2. *Reynolds*, 164, emphasis added.
3. *Reynolds*, 167, emphasis added.
4. *Church of the Holy Trinity v United States,* 143 U.S. 226 (1892).
5. Rockne McCarthy, James W. Skillen and William A. Harper, *Disestablishment a Second Time: Genuine Pluralism for American Schools* (Grand Rapids, Mich.: Christian University Press, 1982), 94.
6. *Pierce v Society of Sisters,* 268 U.S. 510 (1925).
7. McCarthy, Skillen and Harper, *Disestablishment a Second Time.*
8. *Pierce*, 517.
9. *Cantwell v Connecticut*, 310 U.S. 296 (1940).
10. *Sherbert v Verner,* 374 U.S. 398 (1963)
11. *Sherbert*, 406, emphasis added.
12. *Wisconsin v Yoder,* 406 U.S. 205 (1972).
13. *Yoder*, 220.
14. *Yoder*, 215.
15. *Yoder*, 216.
16. McCarthy, Skillen and Harper, *Disestablishment a Second Time.*
17. *Wooley v Maynard,* 430 U.S. 705 (1977).
18. *Thomas v Indiana Employment Security Division,* 450 U.S. 707 (1981).
19. *Thomas*, 741, emphasis added.
20. *Thomas*, 742, emphasis added.
21. *Thomas*, 763.
22. *Thomas*, 764.
23. *United States v Lee,* 455 U.S. 252 (1982).
24. *Bowen v Roy,* 476 U.S. 693 (1986).
25. *Goldman v Weinberger,* 475 U.S. 503 (1986).
26. *Lyng v Northwest Indian Cemetery Protection Assn.*, 485 U.S. 439 (1988).
27. *O'Lone v Shabazz,* 482 U.S. 342 (1987).

28. *Employment Division, Dept. of Human Resources of Oregon v Smith,* 485 U.S. 660 (1990).
29. *Everson v Board of Education,* 330 U.S. 1,15-16 (1947).
30. *Schempp v District of Abington,* 374 U.S. 203 (1963).
31. *Schempp,* 217.
32. *Lemon v Kurtzman,* 403 U.S. 602 (1971).
33. *Tilton v Richardson,* 403 U.S. 672 (1971).
34. *Tilton,* 614.
35. *Tilton,* 614.
36. Wojciech Sadursky, *Law and Religion* (New York: New York University Press, 1982), 4.
37. *Wallace v Jaffree,* 472 U.S. 602, 682 (1985)
38. Paul Weber, *Private Churches and Public Money* (Westport, Conn.. Greenwood Press, 1981).
39. MaryAnn Glendon, "Structural Free Exercise," *University of Michigan Law Review* 90 (1991): 477.
40. Glendon, "Structural Free Exercise," 481.
41. Glendon, "Structural Free Exercise," 481.
42. *Murdock v Pennsylvania,* 319 U.S. 105 (1943).
43. *Murdock,* 140.
44. Glendon, "Structural Free Exercise," 481.
45. Glendon, "Structural Free Exercise," 482.
46. Glendon, "Structural Free Exercise," 482.
47. *Everson,* 19.
48. *Everson,* 44.
49. Glendon, "Structural Free Exercise," 482, emphasis added.
50. Library of Congress Website, www.lcweb.loc.gov/loc/lcib/9806/danpost.html.
51. Sidney Mead, *The Lively Experiment* (New York: Harper & Row, 1965); Thomas Buckley, *Church and State in Revolutionary Virginia* (Richmond, Va.: University Press of Virginia, 1977). This section on the impact of Jefferson's perspective draws from the work of Sidney Mead, Thomas Buckley, Richard Baer, Charles Glenn, Rockne McCarthy, James Skillen and William Harper.
52. Virginia Electronic Library Website, www.etext.lib.virginia.edu/etchbin.
53. McCarthy, Skillen and Harper, *Disestablishment a Second Time,* 83, 86.
54. Note, "Toward a Constitutional Definition of Religion," *Harvard Law Review* 91 (1978): 1620.
55. Mead, *The Lively Experiment,* 135.

Part Two

The Policy Areas

Chapter Three

Curriculum Wars

Nowhere in our culture is the conflict between "freedom of religion" and "freedom from religion" debated more vigorously than in the nation's schools. Cases defending or attacking the legitimacy of prayer in the public school, financing of church schools and the meetings of faith-based groups on public school grounds continue to work their way through state and federal courts every year at every level. For one debate in particular, however, the definition of religion is critical: curriculum.

The curriculum that school children are exposed to is so sensitive because it hits at the tension between parents' desire to be the primary influence on their children and the government's need to influence its citizens. Curriculum issues highlight the need for deciding whether the political or philosophical is ever the equivalent of the religious. Can a school be religiously neutral?

Throughout the 1960s and 1970s the Supreme Court heard a series of "school cases" that, while they served to secure for parents the right to educate children as they saw fit, also firmly entrenched the idea that the state school system had to be devoid of both religious activity and assistance to religious interests in order to maintain religious "neutrality." However, at the same time, the public school systems throughout the country were coming to grips with the fact that families could no longer be depended on to provide the moral foundation necessary for students to become fully responsible citizens. In the 1970s, "values clarification" courses were introduced in the public schools to respond to what some perceived to be a gap in students' ethical development.

Today courses encouraging "critical thinking" of traditional liberal arts subject matters like history are popular; critical thinking curriculum also molds high school units on sexuality and civics. Furthermore, we are seeing a growing interest in educating for character and virtue. For First Amendment purposes, the question is this: can courses emphasizing values or morality be taught in a religiously neutral manner? It depends on what you mean by "religious."

This chapter examines federal court curriculum decisions to uncover the judicial definition of religion as it affects the public schools. Most of the cases have developed from a debate between the religious right and people who believe that "nonreligious" is the same as "religiously neutral." The argument of those that identify themselves as religious is twofold. Initially, parents claimed that if you take God out of the classroom, you are hostile toward religion, and this violates a child's free exercise rights. This perspective, for some, then developed into an establishment clause argument: you do not have to teach about God or Christian moral absolutes in the public school, but then, you must also refrain from teaching moral absolutes of another belief system—in fact, even moral relativism violates the establishment clause.

These arguments require analysis of the character and definition of religion; judges face these arguments with trepidation, preferring to decide cases on any ground other than this definitional one. When the debate centers on the religious nature of beliefs like scientific creationism, evolution and secular humanism, however, the political climate in some states has forced the judges to confront these questions head-on.

Creation Science and Evolution: Belief Systems as Religion?

Throughout the nineteenth and early twentieth centuries, many state school systems refused to teach evolution. In fact, numerous states made it a crime for teachers to introduce Darwinism to the students. Science, particularly the study of the beginning of humanity, was based on Judeo-Christian precepts that included some concept of creation.

However, as the study of evolutionary process became more sophisticated and more accepted by scientists, some schools introduced evolution into their curriculum, often in violation of the law. The ensuing conflict developed into litigation that eventually reached the Supreme Court. For example, in the 1920s fundamentalist Christian revivalism led states like Tennessee and Arkansas to adopt the "monkey laws" prohibiting the teaching of the theory that people evolved from other species of life. The constitutionality of laws like this was upheld by the Tennessee Supreme Court in the Scopes trials of 1927. From 1927 until the early 1960s, the public high schools of Tennessee complied with the law. However, in 1964, Susan Epperson, a high school teacher, was given a biology textbook for use in the coming school year. The textbook contained references to Darwinism, and Epperson petitioned the state court for a declaration stating that the state statute criminalizing her use of the textbook violated the establishment clause of the First Amendment. The state courts of Tennessee refused to void the statute, but the case was appealed to the U.S. Supreme Court. The Supreme Court held that because the statute's purpose was to "blot out" theories that conflicted with the Bible, its purpose was religious, not secular. Therefore, the statute was void.

In response, several states passed laws stating that if schools were going to teach courses that referred to the origin of man, they had to use a balanced approach. If evolution was taught by teachers like Susan Epperson, then, in the name of the students' religious and academic freedom, alternative views like scientific creationism must also be presented. In *McLean v Arkansas* a federal court found one of these statutes to be unconstitutional because it, too, had no secular purpose.[1]

A few years later, the U.S. Supreme Court handed down a decision supporting the federal court in *McLean*. In *Edwards v Aguillard*, the lower court had found without discussion that whether or not creation science was supported by scientific evidence, it was a religious belief.[2] The case then turned on the purpose of the Louisiana Balanced Treatment Act. The court found that the Act violated the First Amendment because it had no secular purpose—the belief it protected was religious, so the Act had a religious purpose. On appeal, the state legislature pointed out that it had gone to great lengths to establish its secular purpose, the academic freedom of students, but the Supreme Court found this to be a sham and sustained the lower federal court's summary judgment overturning the state statute.

What is the issue?

The Supreme Court has held that the government may not establish a religion, nor may it establish a religion of "secularism."[3] However, the meaning of this directive is not clear unless "religion" and "secularism" are defined. In many cases, courts seem to indicate that secularism exists when hostility to religion is exhibited. However, in curricula cases another approach comes to light. Some litigants do argue that schools violate their First Amendment religious freedom rights when books or curricula present ideas that conflict with their religious beliefs. But, other litigants take the argument in a different direction. They say that secularism, itself, is a faith. As such, if it is part of a curriculum in a public school, it violates the First Amendment. The first argument is based on the free exercise clause, the second on the establishment clause.

The arguments can be demonstrated by examining the following statements:

1. Salvation comes from Mohammed, not Jesus.
2. There is no such thing as salvation.

3. I'm OK, you're OK, only you can determine what is right and what is wrong.

Which of these statements, if presented in a public school, would be considered establishing a religion?

From the following cases, it seems that the first statement is clearly a religious statement and cannot be part of the school curriculum. The second statement is hostile to religion, and many judges would find it also to be violative of the First Amendment. But, is the third statement religious? Is it non-religious because it does not mention God, salvation, sin, prayer or other concepts that we traditionally associate with formal religion (the *Davis* definition of religion)? Or, using the *Seeger* definition of religion, does it reflect an ultimate value about humanity?

Throughout the 1970s, federal courts took their cue from *McLean* and *Epperson*, striking down a variety of state methods to force inclusion of alternative explanations of life where evolution was taught. Because the judges in *McLean* and *Epperson* had focused on the *purpose* of the statute, the claim that both evolution and creation science were based on belief systems received little analysis. However, although the nature of religion was not specifically addressed, judges were hard pressed to get away from the argument that students were indeed being indoctrinated into one particular way of thinking. Some courts acknowledged this, others did not.

In *Wright v Houston,* a federal court dismissed a case in which parents sought to enjoin a school district from teaching evolution exclusively and uncritically.[4] In arguing for balanced treatment of creation science, the parents presented two arguments. First, evolution contradicted their religious beliefs. The school's role in discouraging students' belief in creation was a restraint on the free exercise of religion for those students. Second, evolution was part of a religion of secularism. Thus, if taught in public schools, it was establishment of religion. The court refused to accept either argument, saying that, obviously, there was no connection between evolution and religion. The interesting thing, though, is that the court used the definition of religion presented by the Supreme Court in the 1890 case *Davis v Beason*. Religion means relationship to a Creator. Evolution does not mention a Creator; thus, evolution is not a religion.

Despite the reference to an old Supreme Court definition of religion, the court's decision seems to have been molded mainly by pragmatic problems. The judge was particularly troubled by the practical ramifications of holding in any other way. He said that although the equal time approach advocated by the plaintiffs did seem fair,

> virtually every religion known to man holds its own peculiar view of human origins. Within the scientific community itself, there is much debate over the details of the theory of evolution. This Court is hardly

> qualified to select from among the available theories those which merit attention in a public school biology class.[5]

But, this is exactly the point. There is debate about the origin of humanity. And, one's point of view about the origin of life depends on what one holds to be ultimately true. According to the *Seeger* case, this ultimate truth is religion. Even in the scientific community there is no cohesive body of knowledge that all scientists accept as fact regarding how life came to be. Evolutionists must accept some "facts" on faith. So, if one perspective is taught to the exclusion of others, are children receiving "neutral" education? Is the perspective they learn devoid of religion if you use the *Seeger* definition of religion rather than the *Davis* definition? No doubt it would be onerous for the public school system to teach all alternative views of the origin of life, but this difficulty does not change the fact that evolution is based on fundamental assumptions about the world that must be accepted on faith, just as is creation science.

The *Wright* case was not unique in its reliance on the *Davis* definition of religion. As recently as 1992, judges used *Davis* as justification for holding that evolution could not be considered based in religion.[6] The significance of these decisions, however, is that judges are using a definition of religion that relies on the existence of a Creator—a definition rejected by the Supreme Court in 1965.

Secular Humanism

The argument that evolution is based on a theory of life that is foundational, or religious, has never been persuasive to judges. However, soon after the deluge of creation science cases swept the federal courts, the interest of some judges was piqued by the argument that religion did not necessarily mean "relating to God." So, although evolution might not be religion, there could still be other types of curriculum approaches that did reflect religious commitment.

There are two lines of federal court cases that explored this concept throughout the 1980s. Although appellate courts in each line of cases ultimately found that "secular humanism" was not religion, the careful analysis that some of the judges went through to define religion and religious belief is very instructive.

In 1984, a group of children and their parents brought suit against a Tennessee school district, claiming that the textbooks used to teach reading to elementary school students violated the free exercise rights of Christian students. The claim was that the Holt Basic Readings series did the following:

1. taught witchcraft and other forms of magic and occult activity;
2. taught that values are relative;
3. taught disrespect and disobedience to parents;
4. depicted prayer to idols;
5. taught that faith in the supernatural was acceptable for salvation;
6. depicted children who were disrespectful during bible study;
7. implied that Jesus was illiterate;
8. taught that people and apes had common ancestors;
9. taught humanistic values.[7]

Initially, the court found against the parents, saying that the First Amendment did not protect the plaintiffs from mere exposure to offensive value systems or antithetical religious ideas.

> Only if the plaintiffs can prove that the books at issue are teaching a particular religious faith as true (rather than as a cultural phenomenon), or teaching that the students must be saved through some religious pathway, or that no salvation is required, can it be said the mere exposure to these books is a violation of free exercise rights.[8]

So, all counts except number five were thrown out of the case. Then, the court found that the case should be dismissed as to count number five, also, because the poems and stories that the plaintiffs complained about met the court's test of neutrality. The Holt Basic Readings neither advocated a particular religious belief nor expressed hostility to religion. Although the stories, which included Hindu fables and Anne Frank's discussion of religion as believing in "something," did discuss religion, they did not tell the students to believe particular things.

> The plaintiffs correctly reach the obvious conclusion that this poem [the Hindu elephant fable stating as its moral that in theology disputants are often partly right and wrong] meant that each religion described God from its own limited vantage point, based on its incomplete revelation, and that all are only partly right and partly wrong. While that is no doubt the meaning of the poem, there is nothing in the book to suggest that all should subscribe to this way of thinking. The poem is presented for what it is worth. *In the context of the readers taken as a whole, however, it does indeed illustrate the type of religious tolerance presumably requisite to the ideal "world citizen."*[9]

Here, the court's vision of neutrality is clear. Value neutrality occurs when religious belief is not advocated, nor is hostility presented. The school superintendent defended his decision to use the Holt books on the ground that they enhanced reading skills. No proselytizing occurred.

The appellate court overturned the lower court's summary judgment and remanded the case for a decision on the merits. The most significant problem for the appellate court was that the school district had not even tried to accommodate the free exercise rights of the plaintiffs. The least restrictive alternative test had not necessarily been met; a trial on this issue was required.

The problem is, however, that both courts missed the point of the plaintiffs' arguments. The plaintiffs stated that not only is the reading material hostile to their religious belief (a *free exercise* issue) but that the school is teaching an alternative belief system (an *establishment* issue). Neutrality toward religion does not come about merely by eliminating negative connotation of religion, but neutrality requires recognition of the fact that any teaching of ethical values stems from a foundational commitment that parallels a religious commitment. Religion involves salvation and prayer and ritual, certainly, but it is also an ethical system, and alternative ethical systems are not neutral; they *replace* Christianity. As such, they constitute establishment of religion just as much as does the teaching of creationism or Biblical mandates.

The judges in the *Mozert* cases did not develop an answer to this argument. However, at the same time that these cases were decided, Judge William Brevard Hand in Alabama was persuaded that the parallel between secular humanism and theistic religion deserved serious judicial attention.

In May 1982, Ishmael Jaffree sued the Mobile Alabama County School Board seeking a judgment declaring prayer activities in the public school system to be violative of the First Amendment. Douglas Smith and others intervened in the *Jaffree* suit claiming that if prayer were eliminated, their religious free exercise rights would be violated. In addition, they claimed that if an injunction were set forth against the Christian activities in the schools, then an injunction should also be imposed against the religions of secularism, humanism, evolution, materialism, agnosticism and atheism. This complicated case was bifurcated into a school prayer argument, which was taken up first, and a curriculum argument, which never reached the Supreme Court. On the issue of prayer in the schools, the Supreme Court upheld the circuit court's decision finding that prayer violated the establishment clause. The vigor of the litigation, however, and the vehemence of Justice William Rehnquist's dissent shed light on several aspects of the definition of religion and neutrality toward religion.

Initially, the district court had found that the Supreme Court had erred in its earlier decisions that made the establishment clause incumbent on the states. Judge Hand, in a decision that he knew would be overturned, found that historical evidence made it clear that the Framers of the Constitution intended the establishment clause of the First Amendment to apply only to the establishment of a national church. Not only did most of the states have established churches during the 1700s, but the framers of the Constitution themselves, when placed in roles of federal governmental authority, used federal money to subsidize religious activity. Therefore, in keeping with the doctrine of original intent for Constitutional interpretation, state institutions like schools should be allowed to establish religion.

However, given that the case would likely be overturned, Hand cautioned the appellate courts to carefully consider the arguments of the intervenors. He said,

> case law deals generally with removing the teachings of the Christian ethic from the scholastic effort but totally ignores the teaching of the secular humanist ethic. It was pointed out in the testimony that the curriculum in the public schools of Mobile County is rife with efforts at teaching or encouraging secular humanism—all without opposition from any other ethic—to such an extent that it becomes a brainwashing effort. If this Court is compelled to purge "God is great, God is good, we thank Him for our daily food" from the classroom, *then this Court must also purge from the classroom those things that serve to teach that salvation is through one's self rather than through a deity.*[10]

The *Jaffree* case was successfully appealed on the issue of school prayer when the circuit court and the Supreme Court both ignored Hand's historical perspective. The appellate courts used the *Lemon* case to hold that prayer violated the establishment clause because it fostered religion. Then, a new line of cases began on the curriculum issue (referred to as the *Smith* cases). Hand's decision in *Jaffree* lay the groundwork for his careful and lengthy analysis of the nature of religion in the *Smith* cases.

In *Smith*, Judge Hand had to determine whether or not secular humanism was a religion, and, if so, whether it was established in the public school in its philosophy and through the use of certain textbooks.

The complainants said that secular humanism existed in the schools in the following manner:

- God was left out of all discussions of the origin of the universe and out of all discussion of right and wrong;
- teachers and students were required to use books that took the Lord's name in vain;
- students were encouraged to question the authority of parents, and "people in charge" were depicted as those who would use students for their own personal gain;
- students were taught that there were no moral absolutes and that humans were merely a result of a biological process.

The school district defended its approach saying that it was religiously neutral in that it was not hostile toward religion. Secular humanism is not a religion, and even if it is, it is established by the Constitution itself.

The two sides are not merely at cross-purposes, but they are using different perspectives of what religious neutrality is: one argues that religious neutrality occurs when hostility is eliminated; the other argues that neutrality cannot occur until it is recognized that all ethical systems are based in religion of one type or another. These perspectives on religious neutrality stem from different definitions of religion. If religion is purely private faith in God and does not necessarily have implications for all of life, then employment and schooling can be done in a religiously neutral manner as long as God is kept out of them. If, however, one has an integrated view of life, if one believes all decisions in life including employment and schooling issues stem from a foundational belief system, then keeping God out of these decisions rejects theistic religion, but it does not escape being "religious" in a broad sense of the word.

Professor Richard Baer, one of the witnesses in the *Smith* case, explains:

> [i]t is incorrect to assume that one can divide the world neatly into the realm of the religious and the realm of the nonreligious or secular. In a narrow sense of the term religious, this is possible. It is not difficult, for instance, to distinguish between a baptismal service or a bar mitzvah as cultic practices on the one hand and the secular activities of repairing a washing machine or teaching mathematics But many theologians and sociologists argue that in a broader sense religion is that dimension of human culture along with metaphysics which is concerned about questions of the meaning of life and humanity's place in the universe. In this sense Marxist philosophy and other specially secular and humanistic philosophies speak to questions that are religious. I do not mean by this the patronizing view that even atheists secretly believe in God. There are bona fide atheists just as there are bona fide theists. Rather, I refer to the fact that human beings live out their lives in relation to certain basic values that provide meaning and purpose to life. These values function in the life of the atheist in a way that is functionally similar to the way belief in God functions in the life of the theist.[11]

Judge Hand seemed to recognize this problem. In his decision, Judge Hand took testimony from groups of experts to determine answers to the following questions:

- What is the nature of education and the learning process?
- What is a religion?
- Is secular humanism a religion?
- Is secular humanism exhibited in the public schools?

Hand was persuaded by witnesses for both the plaintiffs and the defendants that schooling in the United States involved much more than the mere transmittal of information to students. Teachers and education psychology experts testified that schools were concerned with interpreting facts for students, going so far as to say that the purpose of a school was to develop citizens for a "just world, to develop a humane being."[12] Teachers and textbooks are a significant part of this development; therefore, the testimony of people who deciphered the philosophies outlined in the texts became important to Hand. If the philosophies were religious, they violated the First Amendment. Hand, unlike other judges, recognized that before he could address this question, he had to come to grips with a working definition of "religious."

Referring to the *Seeger* definition of religion, Hand found that under the First Amendment government may not define religion by reference to the validity of the beliefs or practices involved. Content-based definitions result in showing favoritism to some religions. Rather,

> the state must instead look to *factors common to all religious* movements to decide how to distinguish those ideologies worthy of the protection of the religion clauses from those which must seek refuge under other constitutional provision.[13]

Only after you have done this can you distinguish between people's right to define their religious belief and government's right to regulate activities to protect other rights and privileges that are "unrelated to religion." In a footnote, Hand qualified this phrase by saying that if some faiths do not separate actions that are determined by faith and actions that are "unrelated" to religion, government still has the right to supersede religious freedom in order to protect the things that are necessary to have religious freedom: "life, an orderly civilization, peace, protection of the material means for preserving life."[14]

Hand then defined religion as systems of belief that encompassed "fundamental assumptions" about such things as the existence of transcendent reality; the nature of man or the goal of man's existence; and the purpose and nature of the universe. He said that in some belief systems these assumptions were less explicit than in others, but it was important to realize that what often masquerades as "neutral" thought is, in fact, based in foundational belief. This foundational belief is the functional equivalent of religion.

> Whenever a belief system deals with fundamental questions of the nature of reality and man's relationship to reality, *it deals with essentially religious questions*. A religion need not posit a belief in a deity, or a belief in supernatural existence. A religious person adheres to some position on whether supernatural and/or transcendent reality exists at all, and if so, how, and if not, why.[15]

But, only belief that addresses these ultimate values should be protected by the First Amendment.

> A mere "comprehensive world-view" or "way of life" is not by itself enough to identify a belief system as religious. A world-view may be merely economic, or sociological, and a person might choose to follow a "way of life" that ignores ultimate issues addressed by religions. Describing a belief as comprehensive is too vague to be an effective definition under the religion clauses: some religious persons may consider some issues as peripheral that others find central to their beliefs. Diet is one example of this. Another is the devotion of some religions to a non-technological life-style, such as the Amish. A person can be religious for first amendment purposes without having rules and regulations governing every aspect of every day conduct. Equating comprehensiveness with religion results in an overinclusive definition.[16]

Using this definition of religion, Christianity is a religion. But, to Hand, so is secular humanism. Experts at the trial defined secular humanism as a

> creed or world view which holds that we have no reason to believe in a creator, that the world is self existing, that there is no transcendent power at work in the world, that we should not turn to traditional religion for wisdom; rather that we should develop a new ethics [sic] and a new method of moral order founded upon the teachings of modern naturalism and physical science.[17]

The experts explained that secular humanists were not pious, did not believe in transcendent beings, nor did they pray. The belief system was not a dogma, nor a doctrine, but it did express moral values.

Based on the testimony, Hand found that the belief system made statements about the existence of supernatural existence; it sets goals for human existence, and it defined the nature of the universe. The substance of the belief system was that all of reality can be known by the human intellect "aided only by the devices of man's creation or discovery. . . . By the force of logic, the universe is self-existing, knowable. . . . Moreover, man is the product of biology with no spiritual dimension."[18] When Hand applied his definition of religion to the perspective of the textbooks, he found that the books did establish humanism. The home economics textbooks used by the students required them to accept as true the fact that people use the same process in deciding a moral issue that they use in "choosing one pair of shoes over another" and that "the student must determine right and wrong based only on his own experience, feelings and [internal] values."[19] In support of his finding, Hand gave several examples. The home economics textbook *Teen Guide* stated: "Nothing was meant to be. You are the designer of your life. If you want something, you can plan and work for it. Nothing is easy, but nothing is impossible, either. When you recognize that you are the one in charge of your life, you will be way ahead of where you would be if you think of your life as something that just happens to you."[20] Hand pointed out that this encouraged students to believe that only they could decide what is right and wrong.

> [It] is to be contrasted to telling a student that he is responsible for choosing between right and wrong. The latter promotes responsibility . . . The point made is that such teaching leaves out the distinction that must be drawn between what moral values are to be freely chosen and the personal decision involved in applying these values.[21]

Furthermore, another book stated that although six- and seven-year-olds are content to be their mother's daughters or their father's sons, older children probably do not feel this way. "In adolescence people begin defining the world for themselves in their own way. They no longer want to be just someone's son or daughter. They want to be a unique person. They want to discover life and themselves on their own."[22] Judge Hand accepted the testimony of witnesses who explained that this perspective was evidence of a belief system that taught human responsibility was self-directed. This competed with those belief systems that taught there was a divine source for determining the way life ought to be lived.

When texts taught students that they could prepare themselves to make the "right decisions" by working on their self-concept and accepting themselves and believing in themselves, students were indoctrinated into "individualism" to the exclusion of other belief systems. The argument that validity of moral choice is determined by the individual is not religiously neutral. Not only does it undermine traditional religious faiths, but it, itself, is a belief system that competes with faith.

According to Hand, "[t]he emphasis and overall approach [of the books implies] and would cause any reasonable thinking student to infer, that the book[s are] teaching that moral choices are just a matter of preferences, because, as the books say 'you are the most important person in your life.'"[23] Issues of moral choice stem from a person's view of humanity's place in the universe. They are solved by belief systems. If schools teach that these choices are to be solved in an individualistic manner, this is a functional substitute for saying that moral choice ought to be solved by reference to the Bible.

Hand stated that "[t]he highly relativistic and individualistic approach constitutes the promotion of a fundamental faith claim" and "assumes that self-actualization is the goal of every human being, that man has no supernatural attributes or component, that there are only temporal and physical consequences for man's action, and that these results, alone, determine the morality of an action."[24] This belief "strikes at the heart of many theistic religions' beliefs that certain actions are in and of themselves immoral, whatever the consequences, and that, in addition, actions will have extratemporal consequences."[25] Therefore, it is hostile to many religions. "Some religious beliefs are so fundamental that the act of denying them will completely undermine that religion."[26] But, more importantly, "denial of that belief will result in the affirmance of a contrary belief and result in the establishment of an opposing religion."[27] While the state may teach certain moral values, such as that lying is wrong, "if, in so doing it advances a reason for the rule, the possible different reasons must be explained evenhandedly" and "the state may not promote one particular reason over another in the public schools."[28]

On appeal, the circuit court treated Hand's analysis with the same summary dismissal that it employed when it ignored his examination of constitutional history in the *Jaffree* case. The appellate court held that even if secular humanism were a religion, the mere presentation of religious belief did not constitute establishment of religion. Moreover, the books were used to promote critical thinking, independent thought, tolerance of diverse views, self-respect and maturity. Furthermore, one of the major objectives of public education was to inculcate fundamental values necessary to maintain democracy. This was all, obviously, "an entirely appropriate secular effect."[29] This court clearly missed the point of the lower court's discussion when it stated the following:

> The public schools in this country are organized "on the premise that secular education can be isolated from all religious teaching so that the school can inculcate all needed temporal knowledge and also maintain a strict and lofty neutrality as to religion. The assumption is that after the individual has been instructed in worldly wisdom he will be better fitted to choose his religion.[30]

Why Can't It Be Neutral?

Judge Hand's recognition of secular humanism as a religion seems to be based on his belief that all knowledge transmitted in the schools is of social construction. Steven Tipton writes that the meaning of "mutuality, civil spirit, and justice," or the content of our values, are not uniformly self-evident to everyone.[31] This is because our interests conflict, certainly, but it is also because everyone construes meaning within different cultural and moral conditions. Value neutrality does not exist because people are not objective. Our meaning is determined by our experience and our belief.

Even if you say that you want to achieve value neutrality by even-handedly presenting all points of view, you miss the point. The whole concept of value neutrality is, itself, biased towards value systems that are tolerant or based on consensual arrangement. Law professor Stanley Ingber points out that value neutrality

> posits individual criticism and moral choice as values unto themselves. Consequently, a "value-neutral" education would oppose perspectives, such as fundamental Christianity, that advocate imposing values.[32]

Moreover, even though value neutrality or ethical subjectivism sound like the kind of tolerance that schools in democratic society should foster, they contradict themselves. Richard Baer has written that these systems claim that they tell no one what is good or right for them:

> [E]ach individual will have to choose on his or her own individual values. *But this is misleading.* To be specific, if all values are subjective, matters of personal feeling, then we can place no absolute values on things as justice, tolerance of people who hold dissenting views, freedom and equality, or even democracy itself.[33]

The fact is that most Americans do believe that values rest on some foundation greater than simple consensus. There are some things that are fundamentally true and good; we possess certain inalienable rights in addition to whatever those in power might believe or however they might act at any given point in time. What is this foundational truth other than an equivalent to the moral foundation of Christianity, Judaism or Buddhism?

As Baer suggests, moral values come from a worldview. The problem is that when a state school tries to teach students about how they should act, the "should" will always come from some fundamental perspective of what humanity ought to be.

Critics argue that even if what Baer says is true, humanist ethics *should* be taught in public schools because they are rational (based in reason), not religious (based in dogma and revelation). Baer counters this, however, by pointing out that both approaches rest on unprovable assumptions.

> A growing number of philosophers today argue that our use of the terms rational and reasonable are culturally conditioned in a manner that is not altogether different from our use of terms such as good and right. When humanists such as Hook point to the rationality of their own position and to the dogmatic quality of Christian belief, they tend to use the terms rational and reasonable as ideological weapons, making their meanings as much bound to a particular time and place as are our conceptions of the good.[34]

Richard Baer has made the argument that even if values clarification and morality issues like sex education were taken out of the public schools, schools still would not be religiously neutral. All knowledge, even "secular knowledge," is based in foundational belief.

What accounts for the tenacity with which Americans cling to the belief that "secular" equals "neutral?" Baer and other scholars point to Jefferson.

Remember from chapter two that Jefferson believed that his own nonsectarian morality and values were a legitimate foundation for the public life of the nation. He was clear that sectarian religion, the religion of the traditional Christian, should be practiced only in private, not in the public arena that affected civic life. He did support religious freedom, but he expected members of these sects to "behave themselves, to keep to themselves and to stop short of intruding their beliefs and values into the public square."[35]

But, says Baer,

> Jefferson's position is more self-serving than self-evident . . . His Enlightenment faith was just that—a faith commitment, a metaphysical and religious worldview that is no more obviously based on reason than are the beliefs of Christians. Both positions involve convictions that could not be derived from reason as such. They rest on basic assumptions about the nature of reality that can be described as reasonable but that cannot be proven by reason. They rather constitute the foundation for all subsequent reasoning.[36]

It is true, however, that Jefferson did not specifically claim that no religion should affect public life. He was willing to allow the universal religion, the nonsectarian religion, some leeway. In fact, his own university was an example of the kind of moral order that he considered to be acceptable to impose on all citizens. Students at the University of Virginia took chapel and religion classes. However, over time, Jefferson's distinction between sectarian and nonsectarian religion has become, for modern Americans, a parallel distinction between the "religious" and the "secular." This transition occurred throughout the nineteenth century and became solidified with respect to schooling during the Great School Wars of the 1800s.

Former Massachusetts Education Secretary Charles Glenn explains that in the 1840s and 1850s, in New York City and Boston, government schools were accepted by the Protestant majority as public, common and non-sectarian institutions.[37] In these schools, however, the training of students was under the supervision of parents. The supervision included training in values and moral responsibility, as well as Protestant religious training. Because the majority of parents believed, as did Jefferson, that their view was common and universal, they did not consider themselves to be "sects" or "sectarian." They thought they were religiously neutral.[38] Other groups, the minority Catholics, for example, were left out of the perspective of the public schools. They were, however, allowed to have their own, *sectarian* institutions.

As the century wore on, secularization affected many institutions, and God-language was removed from schools. However, although specific references to deity were removed, the schools were still dominated by a pervasive morality that had a distinctly Protestant character. Throughout this whole transition, the schools were considered to be public, religiously neutral, institutions. Minority communities began to bring lawsuits to continue to remove elements of Protestantism from the schools, but did the removal of references to a Christian God truly bring neutrality? Many public schools in this nation continue to look like Protestant schools, while others now look like the belief system of those who replaced the Protestants. The litigants in cases like *Smith* were willing to admit that the schools were not religiously neutral when under Protestant control, but, they assert, the schools are also not religiously neutral while under the control of secular belief.

Today, there is still conflict between Christians, Jews, atheists and those who claim to be simply "secularists." But, of all of these belief systems, are any, really, religiously neutral? It depends on what you mean by religion.

The problem is that the conflict and the litigation continues every day, everywhere. Federal courts continue to hand down decisions stating that the use of folk tales, myths, the world of make-believe and witches and goblins does not foster religion in the public schools. However, schools are entitled to prohibit students from singing "proselytizing songs" in oral communications class even as other students are allowed to make presentations involving explanations of the use of a menorah in the same class. Ceremonial references to deity in civic life, like the pledge of allegiance, are still considered mere "ceremonial deism," not true religion. And, the phrase "In God We Trust" on coins as well as on schools seals or mottoes is considered by the courts to serve a secular, not a religious, purpose. Because we do not agree on what "religion" is, confusion reigns.

Notes

1. *McLean v Arkansas*, 529 F.Supp. 1255 (E.D.Ark. 1982). This chapter is drawn from Julia Stronks and Gloria Stronks, *Christian Teachers in Public Schools: A Guide for Teachers, Administrators, and Parents* (Grand Rapids, Mich.: Baker Book House, 1999), and it appears here with permission.
2. *Edwards v Aguillard*, 482 U.S. 578 (1987).
3. *School District of Abington Township v Schempp*, 374 U.S. 203 (1963).
4. *Wright v Houston*, 366 F.Supp. 1208 (S.D. Texas 1978).
5. *Wright*, 1211.
6. *Peloza v Capistrano Unified School District*, 782 F.Supp. 1412 (C.D. California 1992).
7. *Mozert v Hawkins County Public Schools*, 579 F.Supp. 1051 (E D. Tenn. 1984), 582 F.Supp. 201 (1984), reversed and remanded 765 F.2d 75 (6th Cir. 1985).
8. *Mozert*, 579 F.Supp. 1051, 1053.
9. *Mozert*, 582 F.Supp. 201, 202, emphasis added.
10. *Mozert*, 579 F.Supp. 1051, 1129.

11. Richard Baer, "They Are Teaching Religion in the Public Schools," *Christianity Today* (Feb 17, 1984): 12.

12. *Jaffree v Board of School Comm'rs*, 554 F.Supp. 1104 (S.D. Ala. 1983), aff'd in part, rev'sd in part; *Jaffree v Wallace*, 705 F.2d 1526 (11th Cir. 1983), cert. denied sub nom. *Board of School Comm'rs v Jaffree*, 466 U.S. 926, 953 (1984); *Jaffree v James*, 554 F.Supp. 1130 (1983) aff'd in part, rev'd in part sub nom. *Jaffree v Wallace*, 705 F.2d 1526 (11th Cir. 1983) aff'd, 472 U.S. 38 (1985).

13. *Board of School Comm'rs v Jaffree*, 953, emphasis added.

14. *Board of School Comm'rs v Jaffree*, 979.

15. *Board of School Comm'rs v Jaffree*, 979, emphasis added.

16. *Board of School Comm'rs v Jaffree*, 979, emphasis added.

17. *Board of School Comm'rs v Jaffree*, 961.

18. *Board of School Comm'rs v Jaffree*, 985.

19. *Board of School Comm'rs v Jaffree*, 986.

20. *Board of School Comm'rs v Jaffree*, 986.

21. *Board of School Comm'rs v Jaffree*, 973.

22. *Board of School Comm'rs v Jaffree*, 973.

23. *Board of School Comm'rs v Jaffree*, 986.

24. *Board of School Comm'rs v Jaffree*, 986, 987.

25. *Board of School Comm'rs v Jaffree*, 987.

26. *Board of School Comm'rs v Jaffree*, 987.

27. *Board of School Comm'rs v Jaffree*, 987.

28. *Board of School Comm'rs v Jaffree*, 988.

29. *Board of School Comm'rs v Jaffree*, 962.

30. *Board of School Comm'rs v Jaffree*, 965.

31. Steven Tipton, "Republic and Liberal State: The Place of Religion in an Ambiguous Polity," *Emory Law Journal* 38 (1990): 201.

32. Stanley Ingber, "Religion or Ideology: A Needed Clarification of the Religious Clauses," *Stanford Law Review* 41 (1989): 239.

33. Baer, "They Are Teaching Religion in the Public Schools," 130.

34. Baer, "They Are Teaching Religion in the Public Schools," 131.

35. Baer, "They Are Teaching Religion in the Public Schools," 130.

36. Baer, "They Are Teaching Religion in the Public Schools," 133.

37. Charles Glenn, *The Myth of the Common School* (Amherst: University of Massachusetts Press, 1988).

37. Glenn, *The Myth of the Common School.*

Chapter Four

Employment Practices of Religious Institutions

In the United States the legal relationship between the state as an institution and churches as institutions is fraught with confusion. The First Amendment says, "Congress shall make no law respecting the establishment of religion, or prohibiting the free exercise thereof." But what does this mean about government's relationship to churches, to schools that claim to have a religious foundation, or to Catholic hospitals that choose to not perform abortions?

Clearly, Christians and others who identify themselves with the religious community believe that they ought to be allowed to define their religious institutions in a manner that best reflects the faith that they are called to—but does this mean that the government has no interest in or authority over those institutions? Is freedom of religion the same thing as government "hands off" all institutions that claim a religious foundation? Is it possible for government to be "neutral" with respect to religion? When and how is it legitimate for a state to regulate the employment decisions of a religious institution? This chapter examines Title VII employment discrimination cases to explore the assumptions that federal judges bring to their decisions as they try to define what it means to be religious in the context of employment law.

Church of Jesus Christ of Latter-day Saints v Amos

Title VII of the United States Civil Rights Act makes it unlawful for employers to make employment decisions that are based on an individual's race, color, religion, sex or national origin. With this statute Congress tried to eliminate forms of what the legislators considered to be unjustified discrimination.

To alleviate the tension between the religion clauses and Title VII, Congress enacted a special exemption from Title VII for religious organizations. The statute as originally drafted in 1963 provided that the Civil Rights chapter regarding employment decisions would not apply to "an employer with respect to . . . a religious corporation, association, or society." The provision was very broad. Religious institutions were completely exempt from regulation. However, the exemption that ultimately passed both houses of Congress provided that the chapter would not apply to "a religious corporation, association, or society with respect to the employment of individuals *of a particular religion* to perform work connected with the carrying on by such corporation, association, or society *of its religious activities*."[1] In 1972 the exemption was amended to apply to a "work connected with the carrying on by such corporation, association, educational institution, or society *of its activities*" (removing the word *religious*). This exemption has been upheld by the United States Supreme Court despite the argument that it shows favoritism toward religion.

Although the amendment purports to protect religion, courts still face numerous questions in their interpretation of the statute. Does a religious organization's free exercise right allow it to select employees on the basis of not religion but sex, race and *other* criteria forbidden by Title VII? Lower courts have answered this question in different ways depending on whether the employment decision involved pastoral staff or other types of employees. At this point there is little or no guidance on questions like the following: If I hire a male and a female but my religion says males are the head of the family, may I *pay* him more? Which activities are covered? Is there a difference between religious and secular activities? What about the difference between profit and nonprofit activities? Which institutions are covered? Can seminaries, elementary schools, day care centers, printing centers, bowling alleys and coffeehouses all be considered religious institutions?

The significant thing about this legislation is that it assumes a common understanding of religion in three respects:

- What is a religious *institution* as opposed to a political or philosophical institution?
- What is religious *activity* as opposed to philosophical, moral or even secular activity?

- What is religious *discrimination* as opposed to sexual, racial or just general discrimination?

However, the phrase "religious institution" is not defined in the statute, and the word "religion" receives only this cursory treatment: "The term "religion" includes all aspects of religious observance and practice, as well as belief."

Application of the Statute

In 1987 the United States Supreme Court was faced with a case in which an employee of a gymnasium associated with the Church of Jesus Christ of Latter-day Saints had been fired.[2]

The Deseret Gymnasium in Salt Lake City, Utah was a nonprofit facility open to the public, run by the Mormon Church. The employee, a man named Mason, had been an assistant building engineer at the gymnasium for 16 years. He was discharged in 1981 after failing to qualify for his annual "temple recommend," a certificate stating that he was a member of the Church and eligible to attend its temples.

Mason argued that Title VII as applied to "nonreligious jobs" like janitorial work violated the establishment clause because it favored religious organizations over nonreligious ones. The lower court agreed. However, the Supreme Court ruled that government was allowed to accommodate religious practices in this way. Stressing the non-profit characteristic of the gymnasium, the Court found unpersuasive the lower court's reliance on the fact that Title VII singled out religious entities for a benefit. Moreover, the Supreme Court found that it was too significant a burden on a religious organization to require it, on "pain of substantial liability, to predict which of its activities a secular court will consider religious."[3] Therefore, under this statute, all of a church's activities were to be considered religious. The Court was unwilling to declare some types of activities to be nonreligious when they are performed by a church. Church activity, even if it is janitorial work, is religious activity.

But, what is the nature of this relationship? Is it religious only because it is a church? A private activity by a private group of believers? If so, when does the activity become regulated by the state—when it is public? When it is non-religious? What does this say about the employment decisions of a non-profit group of religious adherents who are not associated with a church? Can they be a religious institution?

In a concurring opinion written to stress the constitutionality of the exemption with respect to nonprofit organizations only, Justice William Brennan emphasized the nature of a community of faith. His opinion illustrates the difficulty inherent in a philosophy that assumes religion can be separated from public life.

> For many individuals, religious activity derives meaning in large measure from participation in a larger religious community. Such a community represents an ongoing tradition of shared beliefs, an organic entity not reducible to a mere aggregation of individuals. Determining that certain activities are in furtherance of an organization's religious mission, and that only those committed to that mission should conduct them, is thus a means by which a religious community defines itself. Solicitude for a church's ability to do so reflects the idea that furtherance of the autonomy of religious organizations often furthers individual religious freedom as well.[4]

Brennan says that if certain activities constitute part of a religious community's practice, then a religious organization should be able to require that only members of its community perform those activities. However, religious organizations should be able to discriminate on the basis of religion only, and with respect to religious activities only. In a perfect world a determination would be made in each case as to whether an activity is religious or secular.

> This is because the infringement on religious liberty that results from conditioning performance of secular activity upon religious belief cannot be defended as necessary for the community's self-definition. Furthermore, the authorization of discrimination in such circumstances is not an accommodation that simply enables a church to gain members by the normal means of prescribing the terms of membership for those who seek to participate in furthering the mission of the community. Rather, it puts at the disposal of religion the added advantages of economic leverage in the secular realm.[5]

To Brennan's credit he does admit that the character of an activity is not self-evident. But, he says that as a result, "determining whether an activity is religious or secular requires a searching case-by-case analysis. This results in considerable ongoing government entanglement in religious affairs."[6] Therefore, these nonprofit institutions should be *completely* exempt from Title VII.

> The fact that an operation is not organized as a profit-making commercial enterprise makes colorable a claim that it is not purely secular in orientation. It makes plausible a church's contention that an entity is not operated simply in order to generate revenues for the church, but that the activities themselves are infused with a religious purpose.[7]

But, what about profit-making institutions? And what about institutions that are not a church but still claim to be religious? They are subject to public regulation because Brennan believes that the economic/public realm is "secular." Religion must be kept "private."

Churches and Employment

As federal courts attempt to apply Title VII of the Civil Rights Act they must determine whether they are dealing with a religious institution; they must determine whether they are faced with religious discrimination; and, pre-*Amos*, they had to determine whether the activity of the institution was a religious activity. In doing so, courts looked to developments at the Supreme Court level, mostly to no avail. These questions have not been fully explicated at the Supreme Court level.

The one area of employment law that seems clear to courts is the relationship between a church and its clergy. Courts consistently maintain a hands-off approach to the hiring of pastoral staff, refusing even to consider whether or not a particular church actually has a theological or "religious" reason for its decision.

Carole Rayburn was a white, female Seventh-Day Adventist with seminary training.[8] In her church, although women are eligible for associate positions in pastoral care, they are not eligible for ministerial internships which require ordination. Rayburn applied for a position as an associate but was turned down. She sued claiming that she had been discriminated against on the basis of her sex, her association with black persons, her membership in black-oriented religious organizations and her vocal opposition to church practices which she believed to be in conflict with Title VII.

Evidence showed that the church position in question involved teaching baptismal and Bible classes, pastoring groups, and occasional preaching. Therefore, the court found the position to be the equivalent of a pastor, and granted summary judgment in favor of the church's claim that it was allowed to discriminate.

The striking thing about this case is the length to which the court was willing to go to protect the church in its selection of its pastor. Despite the ambiguity of parts of Title VII, the lawsuit was not even allowed. In its decision, the court affirmed past decisions that held that the language of ss702 made clear that religious institutions may base relevant hiring decisions on religious preferences. However it said that Title VII did not confer upon religious organizations a license to make those same decisions on the basis of race, sex or national origin (non-religious grounds). If Title VII were the only consideration, even the religious exemption would not protect the church's action.

Then the court found that although Title VII would prohibit any racial or sexual discrimination, the First Amendment would still bar the suit because the state's scrutiny of the choice for pastor would infringe on the church's free exercise of religion and would constitute impermissible government entanglement with church authority.

The court basically held Title VII to be unconstitutional as applied to pastors because it violated the institutional rights of the church. In its analysis the court described the individual's freedom to believe as he or she wishes and stressed that that right applied to churches in their collective capacities which

> must have power to decide for themselves, free from state interference, matters of church government as well as those of faith and doctrine. Ecclesiastical decisions are generally inviolate . . . civil courts are bound to accept the decisions of the highest judicatories of a religious organization of hierarchical polity on matters of discipline, faith, internal organization, or ecclesiastical rule, custom, or law . . . The right to choose ministers without government restriction underlies the well-being of religious community . . . for perpetuation of a church's existence may depend upon those whom it selects to preach its values, teach its message, and interpret its doctrines both to its own membership and to the world at large.[9]

The court said that the role of an associate in pastoral care is so significant in the expression and realization of Seventh-Day Adventist beliefs that *any* state intervention in the appointment process would excessively inhibit religious liberty.

> While it is our duty to determine whether the position of associate in pastoral care is important to the spiritual mission of the Seventh-day Adventist Church, we may not then inquire whether the reason for Rayburn's rejection had some explicit grounding in theological belief . . . in "quintessentially religious" matters . . . the free exercise clause of the First Amendment protects the act of a decision rather than a motivation behind it. In these sensitive areas, the state may no more require a minimum basis in doctrinal reasoning than it may supervise doctrinal content.[10]

Even if the theology was complete subterfuge for gender bias, even if the church's theology did not exclude women, the court would not question the church's hiring decision.

The court stated that although an "unfettered church choice may create minimal infidelity to the objectives of Title VII, it provides maximum protection of the First Amendment right to the free exercise of religious beliefs."[11] However, the court also said that

> Of course churches are not—and should not be—above the law. Like any other person or organization, they may be held liable *for their torts and upon their valid contracts.* Their employment decisions may be subject to Title VII scrutiny, where the decision *does not involve the church's spiritual function.*[12]

This is the crux of the matter. What is the dividing line between a church's spiritual function and its nonspiritual function? It depends on one's definition of religion.

The approach that the court took in *Rayburn* has been confirmed by the Eighth Circuit. In *Scharon v St. Luke's Hospitals*, a female priest was employed by the hospital as a chaplain. When a new supervisor came on board, she was fired because the supervisor believed that she was violating canonical laws.[13] The woman sued the hospital claiming that even if her position was a religious position, and even if the hospital was a religious institution, the accusation regarding canonical laws was pretext for the real motive behind her dismissal.

The court refused to even consider her charge of pretext, dismissing the case on summary judgment. It said that any personnel decisions by church-affiliated institutions affecting clergy are per se religious matters which cannot, under any circumstances, by reviewed by a civil court.

The good thing about courts' attempts to recognize and be sensitive to the identity of the church as an institution is that they see the inappropriateness of a court telling a group of adherents what it ought to believe and how it ought to act on that belief. But, in applying a complete hands-off approach, the courts fall into a trap. Are there never circumstances in which government should regulate employment of a pastor? What if he violates a contract—or if she commits a tortious act? You can see the public/private split of the judges in these situations. Religion is private; religious decisions (like hiring a pastor) ought to be private. But, if the decision is not religious (committing nonreligious discrimination, getting involved in profit activities) regulation can occur because the circumstances are "public."

The problem is that when judges sense an injustice in what a religious institution has done, all they have to do is characterize the institution as "nonreligious" or characterize the activity as "nonreligious" and regulation is appropriate. Unfortunately, not only does this result in inconsistency in the decisions, but it allows judges to decide for themselves what definition of "religion" they want to use. This is the very thing they are trying to avoid when they defer to churches on the issue of hiring a pastor. This is the very thing that *Amos* was intended to minimize.

What Is Religion?

The clear deference that courts give to church hiring decisions for clergy dissolves when courts are faced with other types of employees. In addition, Title VII and its religious freedom exemption can be invoked only after a litigant persuades a court that it has a "religious belief" or an institution persuades a court that it is "religious." This presents two questions: whose definition of religion will courts use, and do courts have a clear understanding of the difference between the secular and the religious?

In *McClure v The Salvation Army*, a federal district court found not only that the Salvation Army engages in religious activities, but also that the Salvation Army itself is a "religion."[14] This finding was based upon the following: "the mission of the organization is to seek the unsaved" and to "secure the commitment of those who are determined to live a Christian life." The Army has major ceremonies that involve marriage, burial and dedication of children, and religious services are held on Sundays. In short,

> [t]hey have all the elements of a Christian witness service They have a preaching part, congregational singing, scripture reading, prayer and the invitation to the unsaved.[15]

Billie McClure worked for the Salvation Army in the late 1960s and her employment was terminated in 1970. She had undergone spiritual leadership training within the church, had become a commissioned officer, and she also performed secretarial duties. McClure claimed that the Salvation Army had employment and personnel practices which violated Title VII's prohibition against gender discrimination. In deciding whether to hear her case the court had to first determine whether or not her activities were religious activities.

In its analysis the court demonstrated some sensitivity to the nature of a religion as expressed by its adherents. The court asked the question

> is welfare work, clerical work, and other normally secular work religious because it is done under the auspices of the religious corporation, i.e., The Salvation Army? Is a religious activity limited to ceremonial or ritualistic functions? Or, does it include support operations which people perform every day in the world of business?[16]

The court decided that all of McClure's work fell under the rubric of "religious activity"; in fact, any work that employees did for the Salvation Army was religious because although some things like secretarial work, or welfare work, might seem "secular," the Salvation Army takes its message "to the people, whether in welfare work, on the street, in a social services building or in a small church."[17]

This case illustrates a broad definition of religion and a broad definition of religious activity. The judge made some effort to explain his decision. Most courts, however, draft a holding without analysis.

In one of the first cases to be decided by a federal court after the 1972 amendments, the district court in Virginia found that the Ku Klux Klan was not a religion. In *Bellamy v Mason's Stores, Inc.* it was undisputed that John Bellamy was fired from his job at a private Virginia corporation solely because he was a member of the United Klans of America. Bellamy filed suit under Title

VII claiming, among other things, that he was the victim of religious discrimination.[18] He stressed the fact that the KKK had ritual, pomp and rites similar to those of various churches, and that it had a specific membership requirement and a specific ideology that functioned as the equivalent of a theology.

Bellamy's argument was rejected out of hand by the court. It dismissed his claim without a hearing on the merits. The court's analysis of the "religion" issue consisted of one sentence.

> [T]he proclaimed racist and anti-Semitic ideology of the organization to which Bellamy belongs takes on, as advanced by that organization, a narrow, temporal and political character inconsistent with the meaning of "religion" as used in ss2000e.[19]

Can eating cat food be an element of a religion? Plaintiff Stanley Oscar Brown brought a suit against the director of the Equal Employment Opportunity Commission (EEOC) when the director dismissed, without hearing, his claim that he had been discriminated against in his employment for exercising his religion (*Brown v Pena*). Brown asserted that his "personal religious creed" required that he eat a particular brand of cat food; this consumption would contribute to his state of well-being and to his overall work performance by increasing his energy. The EEOC dismissed the case because it failed to establish a religious belief "generally accepted" as a religion.

When the case was brought to the federal court the judges cited approvingly the approach taken by the Supreme Court in *Seeger*, emphasizing the fact that there was a difference between a "moral code" and a religion which included a place for a Supreme Being. The court found it significant that throughout case law unique personal moral preferences were excluded from the characterization of religious beliefs. The only finding of fact that the court made or referred to was that

> Plaintiff's personal religious creed concerning Kozy Kitten Cat Food can only be described as . . . *a mere personal preference*, therefore, it is beyond the parameters of the concept of religion as protected by the constitution.[20]

There was no discussion, no hearing, no testimony. There was no evidence to dispute the "religious" base of Brown's claim other than the justices' own beliefs. The court simply relied on its own perspective and on the conclusions of the EEOC director—conclusions also reached without a hearing on the merits of the claim.

The problem with this case is not so much that Stanley Brown was unsuccessful in seeking protection of his religion. Without knowing the circumstances of his employment or termination it is impossible to determine whether injustice was done. However, the fact that the court assumed that the difference between a religion and a moral code is self-explanatory *is* problematic. The following three cases further illustrate judges' willingness to assume that their approach to religion is universal.

In Hawaii, a Protestant missionary named Bernice Bishop left money for the establishment of a school that would hire Protestant teachers to provide children with a good education. That education was to include teaching in morals and in "such useful knowledge as may tend to make good and industrious men and women." One hundred years after the Kamehameha Schools were established they faced lawsuits under Title VII by non-Protestants who claimed that the religious freedom exemption to Title VII did not protect the schools' hiring practices because Protestantism in general was not a religion.[21]

The schools stipulated that there was nothing specific about the subject matter like English, science or mathematics that would make a teacher's Protestantism a necessary qualification for the position. But, despite the admission that there was nothing about Protestantism that affected the content of the teaching, the court found the schools to be religious institutions. The finding that the court made about the "religiosity" of the school was based on the fact that prayers occurred and a general "Protestant" religion course was required for graduation from the school; the donor desired for the children to be instructed in morals by Protestants, and the schools were affiliated with the Bishop Memorial Church which had been established at the time of Mrs. Bishop's death.

This case turned on the finding of religious traditions familiar to the judges. There was no discussion whatsoever about whether or not Protestantism is a religion. But, is "Protestant presence" a religious basis or more of a cultural basis for distinction? This case was overturned by the appellate court on other grounds—the appellate judge did not discuss the "religiosity" of the institution.

Patricia Wessling was a Confraternity teacher in her Catholic church.[22] Two months prior to Christmas she informed her employer, defendant Kroger Co., a meat packing company, that she would require part of December 24 off in order to fulfill her duty to prepare a special Christmas Mass. She was to transport children to and from the mass, set up the church for the program and assist the children during the program. Although she was given permission to have the day off, later the permission was revoked. She left her job early on December 24 to fulfill her church duties and she was fired.

When Wessling sued Kroger for religious discrimination, Kroger defended itself by arguing that although Wessling was a religious person, her activity on December 24 was not religious activity. This argument prevailed when the court held that Wessling

> felt that it was her duty to assist her child's, and other children's education. This sense of duty was important to her and it is important to all mothers who work at developing a close relationship with their children in a moral and religious environment.[23]

However, because her activity on December 24 was voluntary, social and

> far more extensive in time than necessary for religion . . . It was family oriented, a family obligation, not a religious obligation [24]

This statement was the sum total of the court's analysis of the nature of religious activity.

In September 1984, two employees of the Rapides Regional Medical Center were fired because their extramarital affairs with coworkers were "disruptive" to other workers. The plaintiffs sued the Medical Center claiming that they were Baptists, the Medical Center's director was of a different denomination, and that they had been fired because their behavior conflicted with the director's religious views of how personal lives ought to be conducted.

The court took judicial notice of the fact that the Baptist faith embraces the Holy Bible including the Ten Commandments—one of which states: "Thou shalt not commit adultery."

> This being so it would be more than absurd to find that the Baptist faith condones the commission of adultery, much less embraces such a notion as a deep-seated institutional standard. The Court is convinced that plaintiffs could not assert such a thing with even the slightest hint of sincerity.[25]

The court not only ruled in favor of the Medical Center, but it ruled on summary judgment. Moreover, it assessed attorney's fees, costs and a nominal sanction against the plaintiffs for bringing a case so "frivolous" and "unreasonable" on the facts. The court said that under *Yoder*, religious belief was clearly more than personal preference, and it cited approvingly a Fifth Circuit case that required a showing of a "theory of man's nature or his place in the Universe," "sincerity" and an "institutional quality" before a religion existed.[26] In addition, the court cited the *Pena* cat food case as an "enlightening opinion"—had the plaintiffs only understood this case they would never have brought their claim.

However, are *Yoder* and *Pena* cases that clearly distinguish between the religious and the personal? While it is true that Baptists are Christian, is it incomprehensible that some Christian groups take adultery more seriously than others? Isn't it possible that the manager was discriminating against these employees for failing to live out their faith in the way that he believed they ought to?

The last two cases of this section involve government agencies and their chaplains. Although at first glance it seems obvious that government agency chaplains invoke the prohibition against government establishment of religion, the U.S. Supreme Court has held otherwise. These cases illustrate the difficulty that the agencies and courts run into when they try to keep a chaplain but weed out anything "too religious" that the chaplain might say or do.

In *Voswinkel v City of Charlotte* the city and a Baptist Church had entered into an agreement by which the Church would furnish the city with the services of a minister to serve as a full time police chaplain.[27] As defendants, the city and the church argued that the arrangement had a secular purpose and a predominantly neutral effect in accord with the *Lemon* test. However, the plaintiffs, a city taxpayer and a society known as the "American Atheists" were successful in their argument that the city's arrangement gave a preferred position to the Baptist church and resulted in entanglement of religion and the state.

The contract between the church and the city of Charlotte was easily dismissed as unconstitutional; however, the case is interesting because the court ruled as unconstitutional only that part of the agreement that restricted the position to one provided by the church. To have a chaplain was legitimate. For that chaplain to discuss the spiritual and the moral in the performance of his *secular* duties was legitimate. But for the police force to accept a chaplain appointed by a church and then monitor the chaplain's performance with regard to the "religiously-moral" (as opposed to the "secularly-moral") was unconstitutional entanglement.

For example, the contract provided that the police chaplain would:

> 1. Serve as advisor to the Chief in any matter pertaining to the moral, spiritual and mental welfare of police;
> 2. Counsel individual police officers and/or their family members in times of personal crisis, sickness, job-related stress, injury or death;
> 3. Assist officers and family members as necessary in obtaining appropriate outside professional services such as marriage counselors, psychologists, psychiatrists and financial planning counselors;
> 4. Assist police officers and/or medical or rescue personnel in emergencies, disasters or other crisis situations;
> 5. Visit sick or injured police officers at home or in the hospital;
> 6. Provide nonreligious instruction at the Police Academy or at recruit orientation on areas of stress, crisis-handling and services of the chaplain;
> 7. Notification of the family of a police officer or employee of the death of or serious injury to the officer or employee;
> 8. Appearances at civic clubs, churches or other groups as a public relations representative of the Police Department.
>
> The Police Chaplain shall not engage in religious instruction nor conduct any service of religious worship while wearing the uniform of his office or while acting in his capacity as Police Chaplain. The Chaplain may provide religious guidance to any police officer or other person he is counseling when he is specifically requested to do so by the officer or other person being counseled.[28]

The court held number one to be unconstitutional and the last paragraph to be unconstitutional, but felt that the chaplain could perform the rest of the "secular" duties. The chaplain provided by the church was an ordained minister with substantial background in emergency counseling. He testified as to his understanding of his duties under the contract by stating that while the chaplain was "not to engage in religious instruction nor conduct any service of religious worship," he "may provide religious guidance to any police officer or other person he is counseling when he is specifically requested to do so by the officer or other person counseled."[29]

The defendants argued that provision for "spiritual" and "moral" needs is not inconsistent with a "purely secular" counseling function. The court accepted this argument stating that concern for such matters "is not the exclusive province of the religious; *it may be that even atheists have spiritual interests.*"[30] So the spiritual and the moral are not religious.

The court was troubled by the fact that although the city sincerely tried to secularize the police chaplaincy it was unable to do so. The chaplain was free to give religious guidance when requested but was not to engage in religious instruction. The court said that without the limiting clause the contract was direct establishment of the Baptist creed in the police department. However, with the prohibition, the contract created the potential for entanglement in religious matters that the Supreme Court cautions against.

> If the Police Chief is to see to it that the prohibition on religious activity is honored, then he must make the Solomonic distinctions between the religious instruction that the contract forbids and the moral and spiritual advice that the chaplain was hired to provide . . . he must decide if the resulting advice was religiously moral rather than secularly moral in content.[31]

But, the solution, for the court, was to remove the governing function of the police chief (the state) and to allow a chaplain to be moral but not too religious.

Can the chaplain's morality be religiously neutral? The court acknowledged that the establishment clause requires neutrality between competing religions and between religion and nonreligion. However, in its attempt to define what it meant to be neutral it used its own understanding of "religion" and "secularity" which involved assumptions that might violate others' understanding of these terms. Unfortunately, even in its effort to be sensitive to the issue, the court was not even able to see its own assumption.

Franklin Baz was hired as a chaplain for the VA medical center in Danville, Illinois. He was in charge of various activities for the center's patients, including the Sunday evening "sung service." Baz was fired from his job because he conducted his activities with too much Christian evangelism which was interpreted by his boss to be proselytizing.

Baz's argument at trial was that he had been hired so that he might practice his religion in the service of a secular employer and was fired when his employer did not approve of his doing exactly that. In addition, Baz argued that the

VA, through its rules and regulations governing the conduct of VA chaplains, has impermissibly established an institutional theology at VA facilities. The VA violated the establishment clause of the First Amendment when it took steps to limit and restrict the manner in which Baz "could pray with patients, preach, and also limited the content of his sermons."[32] Baz said that he was fired because he would not conform his ministry to the dictates of the VA-sanctioned institutional theology.

The appellate court found that there was no evidence that the VA had an institutionalized theology at Danville, but rather, it had instituted an "ecumenical approach" to its chaplaincy with special attention to the needs of its patient population.

As the lower court had described it,

> [t]he plaintiff saw himself as an active, evangelistic, charismatic preacher while the chaplain service and the medical staff saw his purpose as a quiescent, passive listener and cautious counselor. This divergence in approach is illustrated by the plaintiff's listing "twenty-nine decisions for Christ" in his quarterly report of activities of the Veterans Administration. It was one of the matters pointed out to the plaintiff by [his boss] as unacceptable conduct on the part of the Veterans Administration chaplain.[33]

The case could have been resolved simply as a failure to perform duties in the manner required by a superior, but the appeals court went further, claiming that Baz had no right to impose his religious perspective on patients who did not want to listen to him. He was to perform his chaplain duties in a secular manner. The court tried to be sensitive to the idea that a government facility does not have to be hostile to religion in order to be neutral; thus, having a chaplain was allowed. However, in its attempt to be neutral the court allowed the facility to describe its own ecumenical approach as non-sectarian but Baz's approach as religious.

All of these cases illustrate that the definition of religion involves more than simply deciding which faiths ought to be covered under the First Amendment. In addition, courts determine which types of activities are religious and which are secular. This, too, involves a definition of religion but the definitional issue is a subtle one. If my definition of religion suggests that counseling is a secular activity, then the definition of religion is even more limiting than if I said Santeria is not a protected faith.

Claiming counseling to be a secular activity brings us right back to the belief-action dichotomy. Does this mean that a religious adherent may believe what he or she chooses, but when he or she counsels, even as a chaplain, it is secular behavior which is regulated outside the parameters of the First Amendment? It is a complicated question.

Businesses as Religious Organizations

The previous sections examined judges' consideration of the nature of religion; this section considers institutions that claim to be religious but function in the business world.

King's Garden was a non-profit interdenominational religious and charitable organization. Its activities included a number of ministries whose basic goal was to "share Christ world wide." However, as a licensee of a radio station it was under the jurisdiction of the Federal Communications Commission. When the FCC required King's Garden to submit a report of its hiring policies, King's Garden filed for a judicial review of the agency's order.[34]

In 1974, ten years prior to the U.S. Supreme Court's rulings in *Amos*, the D.C. Court of Appeals held that the Title VII religion exemption was unconstitutional under the establishment clause because it gave religious organizations too great a preference. Although *Amos* ultimately ruled the exemption as constitutional, the concerns of the court in King's Garden shed light on the difficulties with this statute.

The court said that in covering all of the activities of any religious corporation, association, education institution or society,

> the exemption immunizes virtually every endeavor undertaken by a religious organization. If a religious sect should own and operate a trucking firm, a chain of motels, a race track, a telephone company, a railroad, a fried chicken franchise, or a professional football team, the enterprise could limit employment to members of the sect without infringing the Civil Rights Act. If owned and operated by a nonreligious organization, the enterprise could not use sectarian criteria in hiring, except where the particular job position carried a bona fide occupational qualification of a religious character.[35]

The court said that it could not conceive what secular purpose was served by the "unbounded exemption enacted in 1972. As for primary effect, the exemption invites religious groups, and them alone, to impress a test of faith on job categories, and indeed whole enterprises, *having nothing to do with the exercise of religion*."[36]

Because the First Amendment demands neutrality of treatment between religious and nonreligious groups

> [i]t is conceivable that there are many areas in which the pervasive activities of the State justify some special provision for religion to prevent it form being submerged by an all-embracing secularism *but it hardly follows that the state may favor religious groups when they themselves choose to be submerged, for profit or power, in the all-embracing secularism of the corporate economy*.[37]

The court also commented on the public aspect of this business.

> As Congress is fully aware, broadcasting under the Communications Act is not an altogether private industry. Federally licensed broadcasters as are public trustees. The premise of the . . . argument is that King's Garden's radio station is an integral part of the sect's missionary structure. From this premise King's Garden concludes that the Commission's fair employment rules tamper unconstitutionally with the sect's hierarchy, membership policy, and administration. The conclusion is based on the recognized doctrine, noted earlier, that the internal affairs of a church are immune from public regulation under the Free Exercise Clause. But the argument's premise is defective. A religious sect has no constitutional right to convert a licensed communications franchise into a church. A religious group, like any other, may buy and operate a licensed radio or television station. But, like any other group, a religious sect takes its franchise burdened by enforceable public obligation.[38]

These sections highlight troubling questions. What is it about the character of a church that makes it different from a business? If you acknowledge that all of life is religious, including business life, for some groups, then where do you begin to draw lines between what activity should or should not be protected? Is economic life public, and thus, always secular?

Two years after *Amos* was handed down, the Ninth Circuit Court of Appeals issued an injunction prohibiting an employer from requiring that all employees attend a devotional service during the work week.[39] Although the Townley Engineering Company paid the employees for their attendance, and made it clear to the employees before hiring them that attendance would be mandatory, the court found that the practice violated Title VII.

In making its determination, the court conceded several facts: Jack and Helen Townley, in founding their company, made a covenant with God that their business would be a "Christian, faith-operated business." They were "born again believers in the Lord Jesus Christ" who were "unable to separate God from any portion of their daily lives, including their activities at the Townley company."[40] The company reflected this commitment by enclosing a Gospel tract in all outgoing mail, printing Biblical verses on all company invoices and other documents, giving financial support to churches and missionaries and holding devotional services once a week during office hours.

However, the court found without discussion that Title VII was not intended to protect religious institutions in the business world. The court said that the Civil Rights statutes required corporate owners to excuse employees with religious objections from attending devotional services at work, and the court held that this did not unduly burden the owners' free exercise rights. The corporation was "secular" in that it was not affiliated with a church, and therefore, was not "religious." Moreover, Townley's accommodation of employees who objected to the services would not cause undue hardship to the company because in the court's opinion, spiritual hardship did not have an adverse impact on the conduct of the business. Townley argued that releasing employees from devotions would have a chilling effect on his mandate to share with all of his employees the spiritual aspects of the company. This argument failed because to the court "chilling" was irrelevant if it had no effect on the company's "economic well-being."[41] Finally, the court concluded that even if ending mandatory attendance at devotional services would have an impact on the Townleys' religious practice, it would not be an unreasonable or extreme impact.

In the last paragraph of the decision, the court confused the issue by amending the decision of the lower district court. The lower court had enjoined mandatory services for all employees, whether or not the objections to the services were "religious" in nature. The appellate court said that the goal of the Civil Rights statutes was to end religious discrimination and that therefore, the Townleys had only to excuse those employees who made *religious* objection to the services. Unfortunately, the court failed to explain how litigants were to distinguish between religious objections and those objections based merely on conscience or moral codes.

The problem here is that any effort by courts to distinguish between religious and nonreligious practice will not make sense to communities that perceive life as an integral whole. The Townleys viewed all of life in religious terms, rather than divided into areas clearly religious or nonreligious. The dissenting judge, Justice Noonan, recognized this when he said the following:

> The . . . court appear[s] to assume that there must be a sharp division between secular activity and religious activity. Such a sharp division . . . such a dichotomy, is a species of theology. The theological position is that human beings should worship God on Sundays or some other chosen day and go about their business without reference to God the rest of the time. Such a split is attractive to some religious persons. It is repudiated by many, especially those who seek to integrate their lives and to integrate their activities. Among those who repudiate this theology is the Townley Manufacturing Company.[42]

Ironically, Justice Noonan is the author of a book on religious freedom jurisprudence in which he defines religion as belief in God.[43]

This chapter illustrates that the definition of religion is even more complex than simply determining whether a minority group's view is religious. In addition, judges distinguish between religious and secular activity, religious and secular discrimination, and religious and secular institutions. The assumption that religion is a private belief results in the conclusion that public activity is, and must be, secular. If the public sphere is secular, it can be regulated, but this violates the Supreme Court's desire to be sensitive to the fact that belief and action are intertwined. Decisions like *Amos* illustrate this sensitivity, but they do not resolve the definitional issue. And, the questions that *Amos* leaves open are critical.

Notes

1. Title VII of the Civil Rights Act of 1964, ss 702, 42 U.S.C. ss 2000.
2. *Corporation of the Presiding Bishop of the Church of Jesus Christ of Latter-day Saints v Amos*, 483 U.S. 327 (1986).
3. *Amos*, 336.
4. *Amos*, 344.
5. *Amos*, 344.
6. *Amos*, 344.
7. *Amos*, 344.
8. *Rayburn v General Conf. of Seventh-Day Adventists*, 772 F.2d 1164 (4th Cir. 1985).
9. Rayburn, 1167.
10. Rayburn, 1169.
11. Rayburn, 1170.
12. Rayburn, 1170.
13. *Scharon v St. Luke's Hospitals*, 929 F.2d 360 (8th Cir 1991).
14. *McClure v The Salvation Army*, 323 F Supp. 1100 (1971); aff'd 460 F.2d 553 (1972).
15. *McClure*, 1102.
16. *McClure*, 1106.
17. *McClure*, 1106.
18. *Bellamy v Mason's Stores, Inc.*, 308 F.Supp 1025 (1973); aff'd 508 F.2d 504 (4th Cir. 1974).
19. Bellamy, 1126.
20. Bellamy, 1385.
21. *EEOC v Kamehameha School/Bishop Estate*, 780 F.Supp 1317 (D. Hawaii 1991)(reversed on other grounds).
22. *Wessling v Kroger*, 554 F.Supp 548 (E.D. Michigan 1982).
23. *Wessling*, 552.
24. *Wessling*, 552.
25. *McCrory v Rapides*, 635 F.Supp 975 (W.D. La. 1986).
26. *Brown v Dade Christian Schools*, 556 F.2d 310 (5th Cir. 1977).
27. *Voswinkel v City of Charlotte*, 495 F.Supp 588 (W.D. North Carolina 1980).
28. *Voswinkel*, 591.
29. *Voswinkel*, 593.
30. *Voswinkel*, 596.
31. *Voswinkel*, 596.
32. *Baz v Walters*, 782 F.2d 701 (7th Cir. 1986).
33. *Baz*, 703, citing 599 F.Supp 614, 617 (C.D. Ill. 1984).
34. *King's Garden v FCC*, 498 F.2d 51 (D.C. Cir. 1974).
35. *King's Garden v FCC*, 54.

36. *King's Garden v FCC,* 54.
37. *King's Garden v FCC,* 57.
38. *King's Garden v FCC,* 57.
39. *EEOC v Townley Engineering,* 850 F.2d 610 (9th Cir 1988).
40. *EEOC v Townley Engineering,* 612.
41. *EEOC v Townley Engineering,* 616.
42. *EEOC v Townley Engineering,* 625.
43. John Noonan, *The Lustre of Our Country: The American Experience of Religious Freedom* (San Diego: University of California Press, 1998).

Chapter Five

Regulation and Funding of Social Service Organizations

Agencies that provide social services to citizens of the United States are subject to a wide variety of governmental regulatory laws. Employment practices are regulated by civil rights laws and labor laws, health and safety standards protect employees and consumers of the agencies, tax codes determine which agencies must contribute to the public coffer and zoning ordinances determine where the agencies may set up shop. But, what is the difference between the government's regulation of a charitable organization and the regulation of a *religious,* charitable organization? If a religious, non-profit group provides social services to society, should it be exempt from regulatory law? May it receive funding from the government? Does the law distinguish between the "religious" activity of a religious organization and its "secular" activity? If so, what makes up the basis for this distinction?

This chapter examines the assumptions about religion that federal courts bring to their decisions as they apply the First Amendment to government policies that regulate or fund social service agencies. The first section of this chapter focuses on the licensing requirements and regulations affecting day care centers as a tool for exploring the definition of religion as it affects one type of social service agency.

The second section focuses on the courts' use of the phrase "pervasively sectarian." More and more, government welfare reform proposals are taking into account the role that nongovernmental organizations have played in helping people to fulfill their own varied responsibilities in life. Churches, soup kitchens, homeless shelters, day care centers, domestic violence safe houses, federal, state and city funded agencies that serve low-income citizens in a variety of ways are all considered to be an important part of our social fabric. But, if government chooses to fund these agencies, may it (must it) differentiate between religious and nonreligious agencies? Does government establish a religion if it includes religious agencies in its proposed social welfare reforms? If so, how do courts determine which agencies are religious and which are merely charitable or moral?

Licensing Requirements and Regulation: *Forest Hills Early Learning Center v Grace Baptist Church and the State of Virginia*—A Decade of Conflict

Since 1948 the state of Virginia, like many states, has required all childcare center operators to obtain licenses and to comply with specific health and safety regulations. For years, the standards were fairly limited in scope. Until the 1970s there was almost no litigation in this country regarding either the free exercise argument that sectarian day care centers must be exempt from regulation or the establishment argument that arguably forbids exemption.

Throughout the 1970s, however, women entered the work force in larger numbers and more and more children began to be brought up in single parent homes. The demand for safe, regulated childcare increased, and states responded by setting detailed, mandatory standards that covered health and safety, but also discipline of children, parental involvement or control over the center, and sometimes even curricular programs.

In 1976 the Virginia Department of Welfare passed comprehensive child care regulations. Area churches responded by stating that their religious beliefs would not permit them to apply for or accept licensing or regulations. The licensing usurped the authority of God over the church, and regulations interfered with a function (childcare) which was an integral part of the church's religious ministry. The Virginia legislature then passed an exception to the regulations, saying that any child care operation offered by a religious institution would be exempt from both the licensing requirement and all but the most basic safety requirements.

When the exemption was passed, nonsectarian childcare centers sued the state claiming that the statute violated the establishment clause. Because the nonsectarian centers suffered financially in the market place as they competed with sectarian centers that did not have to make expensive adjustments to comply with the regulation, the state sponsorship of the sectarian centers amounted to state establishment of religion. The nonsectarian centers perceived state support of sectarian centers based on the following:

- The sectarian centers were completely relieved of official state regulation in the areas of licensing, program, insurance, financial resources and management, staff qualification, and internal administration following licensing, while the nonsectarian centers were subject to extensive regulation in these areas, enforceable by state agency inspection and legal sanctions.
- Sectarian centers had "only limited disclosure and certification requirements and no sanctions exist for violation."
- In the areas of health and safety, "sectarian centers are also relieved of a wide range of regulatory standards which apply to nonsectarian centers." Sectarian centers were subject only to those health and safety standards "already applicable to the general population through local and state fire, safety and sanitation codes." Nonsectarian centers were subject to "state level inspection and enforcement mechanisms" while sectarian centers were subject only to the "inspection and enforcement powers of local health, welfare and fire departments acting on complaints of parents."[1]

A lawsuit challenging the state's exemption for religious centers was filed in 1979 and was litigated for over a decade. Initially, the lowest federal court held that as a matter of law the statutory exemption was constitutional because the First Amendment permitted, and may have even required, that the religious freedom of these organizations be protected. Religious freedom meant government "hands-off" the religious institution.

On appeal, however, the Fourth Circuit Court of Appeals held that there was nothing wrong with general regulation of religious institutions. If the center wanted to put forth a free exercise claim it had to show that the exempt activities themselves were sufficiently "central" to the organization's faith identity. The court said that the fact that an activity was a "good work" of a religious institution did not make it a "religious" activity. Core religious practices like prayer, worship and ritual were entitled to protection, but if an organization wanted exemption from licensing and general regulations, it would have to show that the licensing process itself and the regulations interfered with its core religious identity. At that point, the state would still have the chance to deny religious exemption based on a compelling state interest. The circuit court sent the case back down to the district court for findings regarding the "religious" versus the "secular" activities of the sectarian child care centers.

The district court's 1987 decision phrased the new issue as follows:

> whether and to what extent free exercise rights expressed in exempt activities would be burdened by the application of the state's minimum standards for licensed child care centers to church-run centers and, if so, whether that burden is nevertheless justified by a compelling state interest.[2]

Its attempt to draw a line between religious and secular activities was summarized in one paragraph:

> Regarding the issue of whether the operation of childcare centers by class members is a part of their respective ministries, this Court concludes that *while the class members may characterize this activity as a part of their ministries, the Court is not bound to accept this characterization*. Applying the tests set forth by the Fourth Circuit, the Court concludes that the operation of childcare centers by these sectarian institutions is a secular, and not religious, activity. Therefore, the operation of such centers is not entitled per se to free exercise protection. The operation of a childcare center is not an "active expression" of the churches' particular beliefs regarding their ministering to their children but is merely incident to such "active expression."[3]

The court's analysis rested on the observation that some religious child care agencies had no resistance to the state licensing regulation which was "probative" of whether or not child care centers were an expression of "centrally held religious beliefs." Furthermore, because the church child care centers developed in the 1970s, the court said that their existence was a response to the growing number of women in the work force, which was a "secular" not a "religious" need.

Here, the court adopts a vision of religion that indicates that faith is a private, core belief. As soon as that belief affects the public realm, the economic realm, it is not religious, but rather becomes secular.

However, the court then proceeded to cover all bases. It said that even if the operation of a child care center *was* a religious activity, the compelling state interest in protecting the health and safety of children justified the licensing requirement. Moreover, the licensing request was the least restrictive means for protecting this interest. For example, the information requested by the state on its one-page financial disclosure form "represents a minimal intrusion into the financial affairs of one secular activity conducted by a church—its child care center—while serving the purpose of assuring a center's financial ability to comply with the standards."[4] Because the intrusion was limited, and the state concern significant, religious interests must bow to the government.

Then, the court went on to apply this rationale to the way in which the centers were run. The churches objected that the minimum curricular standards would permit the state to impose program content requirements that reflect a "secular humanism philosophy" incompatible with their religious beliefs. Without discussion of the content of secular humanism versus the churches' belief systems, the court concluded that the curricular requirements did not regulate substantive content but rather emphasized physical and mental development of children by "encouraging centers to provide a broad range of activities, without directing the content or substance of such activities."[5] The churches disagreed, saying that the requirement to include rhythm, music and dancing in the daily activities of its program, and the requirement to promote "positive self-concept" could conflict with their vision of dancing as sinful, and man as depraved. However, the court asserted that there was no basis to conclude that the state would interpret its regulations in such a way as to conflict with the programs of the church-run institutions.

The churches also argued that the "good moral character" hiring regulation enabled the state to compel a church-affiliated child care center to hire someone the church felt lacked good moral character. For example, given the fact that the state had a policy against discrimination against homosexuals in public school employment, could the state compel a church to hire a homosexual? The court said that because the day care received no public funding, its hiring practices were protected; this point should not be of concern.

Finally, the state also required that the child care center refrain from corporal punishment. The churches argued that they should be in charge of meting out discipline in accord with their teaching. The court said that

> [b]ecause the operation of a childcare center is a secular activity even when conducted by a church, the state may require a church-affiliated childcare center to refrain from corporal punishment. Even if the activity were religious, the state had a compelling state interest in protecting young children in care away from home from physical and emotional harm . . . . Where religious practices risk or endanger the health and well-being of members of society, the state may regulate such practices to avoid the adverse health consequences.[6]

However, this quote illustrates the problems faced here. If the state can regulate to protect "health" and "well-being" of society using the compelling interest test, it can easily substitute its vision of the good society for that of any given religion or faith community. It is precisely this majoritarian regulation of faith commitments that the First Amendment was designed to protect against. There may well be limits to what religious organizations may do to children, but when a court first claims that child care is not religious in nature, its second claim that even if it were religious the compelling interest of the state justified regulation is a foregone conclusion.

One year after the district court held the licensing and regulatory provisions applicable to religious day care despite the legislated exemption, the Supreme Court handed down *Amos* (see chapter four), the employment case decision that upheld as constitutional a federal statute that gave religious institutions an exemption from civil rights employment laws. The rationale of this case hinged on the Court's recognition that the separation of "religious" activities from "secular" activities of a church-related institution did damage to the self-definition of a religious organization.

The *Amos* case was handed down just as the federal district court set forth its condemnation of the Virginia exemption for religious day care centers. Within weeks the Virginia case was appealed once again to the Fourth Circuit asking the appellate court judges to use *Amos* to claim the exemption to be constitutional. In a two-page decision, the circuit court did exactly that. Ten years after the litigation had begun, the church-run day care centers were free from governmental regulation.

Since the decisions of *Amos* and *Forest Hills*, numerous other federal courts have upheld state laws that exempt from regulation childcare agencies integrally related to a church. Courts do this easily, without analysis. For example, in *Forte v Coler*, the court granted summary judgment in favor of religious child care centers, holding without discussion that "[although church related facilities] still must comply with minimum local health, sanitation, and safety ordinances and Florida's personnel screening requirements, they are not subject to the broad ranging regulations other child care facilities must conform to."[7] The assumption is that church activities are religious, so they may be exempt from the law.

However, there are still unanswered questions that affect the identity of religious institutions. First, what does it mean to be a religious organization? In the arena of day care agencies, the relevant legislation involves sectarian centers. There is little legislation that relates to a center that is not sectarian, but wants to be considered religious, qualifying under these exemptions. This does not mean, however, that these cases will not develop. As chapter four illustrated, in the area of employment rights the nature of "religious institution" has been litigated for years, and courts still fluctuate between being willing to create this definition themselves versus letting institutions define their own "religiousity."

Also, although the courts determine that the First Amendment establishment clause analysis does not *prohibit* states from exempting religious institutions from generally applicable law, will courts *require* states to grant exemptions if the legislators are not inclined to do so voluntarily? It depends.

Given the concerns in *Amos*, that issue-by-issue free exercise litigation would entangle the courts in "religion" and would threaten the self-identity of the religious mission of an institution, it would seem reasonable to conclude that the courts would require states to grant some general "religiously" based exemption to individuals and groups claiming that state laws caused them to violate their faith. In the past, courts have done exactly that, using the "compelling state interest" standard as the test for legitimate state regulation. However, at this point the law and the standards to be used are somewhat unsettled. In the 1990 *Smith* case, the United States Supreme Court determined that in some cases the compelling state interest standard was inappropriate when an individual or group asserted a claim based solely on the free exercise clause of the First Amendment.

Recall that in *Smith*, Scalia wrote that the right of free exercise does not relieve an individual of the obligation to comply with a valid and neutral law of general applicability just because he or she thinks the law constricts activity that a religion requires. In determining whether or not the legislation was "valid" the Court asked not if it was "compelling," but if it was "reasonable." Furthermore, the Court acknowledged that leaving accommodation of religious expression to the legislative, political process could place minority religions at a disadvantage. As long as the law was "neutral," not distinguishing between religions, it was legal. Calling this the unavoidable consequence of democratic government, the Court stated that it was preferred to a system in which each conscience is a law unto itself.

The critical point here is that for some judges laws are considered to be religiously neutral if they do not specify a particular religion. For others, neutrality occurs only as long as government does not distinguish between religions. And for still others, neutrality exists only when all organizations, whether or not religious, are treated the same. *Smith* returns us to the problems embedded in the belief/action dichotomy. First, how do we or should we separate religion from philosophical or moral belief? Second, is it legitimate to say that "only beliefs are protected; actions are protected only if the majority agrees to it?"

Applying the *Smith* Case

The Salvation Army has been recognized as a church by federal courts since 1971. In 1979, New Jersey enacted a Rooming and Boarding House Act in response to public outcry regarding the unsafe conditions of these institutions. The Act regulated physical safety of the residents, but it also instituted a bill of rights for people living in these rooms. The bill of rights particularly emphasized the privacy and the freedom of the residents. When the Salvation Army sought an exemption from state requirements regulating boarding houses, the Third Circuit Court of Appeals determined that the religion clauses of the First Amendment did not protect this religious agency from state regulation.[8]

The Salvation Army ran voluntary rehabilitation centers designed to renew and rehabilitate homeless and socially troubled men through spiritual teaching, counseling and work therapy. These centers fell under the jurisdiction of the Act. The centers consisted of mandatory "work therapy" in the Salvation Amy's thrift stores which funded the centers but also served as a means of helping the residents take a place in society. The residents did not receive salaries but did receive a gratuity. They were required to engage in "spiritual activities" including religious services and spiritual counseling. In addition, visitors were restricted, and meals and other activities were part of the communal nature of the center so socialization was regulated. The residents were free to leave at any time, but this structure still violated the Act's bill of rights.

When the Act was passed, the Salvation Army asked for exemption from all parts of the Act other than those related to the physical safety of residents. The reason for the exemption request was that these centers were not "secular" or "social," but rather they were central to the religious mission of The Salvation Army.

The court, relying on *Smith*, found that because the Act was not directed toward religious activity, and thus was "neutral" toward religion, regulation was not subject to a free exercise clause challenge. The court would not require the state to grant exemptions for religious organizations. The problem is that the Supreme Court in *Amos*, just five years earlier, had specifically denounced this separation of religious activities from secular activities in a religious institution.

Salvation Army was not a day care case, but if day care cases prior to *Salvation Army* and *Smith* are examined, the position judges will take in the future seems clear. Even before *Smith*, judges found in favor of the state when sectarian day care schools challenged state regulations that interfered with them. The courts used compelling state interest to justify the regulation. Post-*Smith*, the test moves from "compelling" to the lower threshold of the "reasonableness" of the state's concern. The following case, using the compelling standard, illustrates the difficulty religious institutions will have in arguing that the First Amendment means government "hands off" religious agencies.

In *North Valley Baptist Church v McMahon* a religious group that operated a child care center challenged a state law that refused to exempt it from licensing or state regulations. The court held that the California ChildCare Facilities Act did not foster excessive governmental entanglement with religion even though it did regulate the agency.

Moreover, the regulations did not affect religious objectives of groups operating child care centers because "the licensing scheme left unregulated every aspect of the preschool's operations which was religious in nature."[9] Here, again, you see a separation of the religious from the secular, without discussion of what that means.

The primary issues in this case were the licensing requirement and the state's concern about the nature of discipline in the center. The Act prohibited corporal punishment, which conflicted with the teachings of the Baptist church. The preschool operated consistently with the principles and beliefs of the church. Preschool staff had to be members of the Church, and they were expected to conduct themselves in an appropriate "Christian manner." Teachers were to integrate Biblical teachings into all aspects of instruction. Although the church believed "that the primary responsibility for the upbringing of children lies with parents," in order to instill "learning and self-control," the center implemented a structured discipline policy including spankings.[10]

The discipline policy was set forth in the center's handbook, and all parents of children at the school signed authorization forms indicating that they supported the school in its discipline policy.

When the center opened, it applied for and received a license from the state. However, over the period of a decade the pastor of the church along with the Board of Deacons began to believe that the state government had "crossed the invisible line" between church and state and had begun to "eliminate the historical and constitutional right of the church to minister to the needs of the people without interference from government."[11] Accordingly, he claimed that "renewing of our preschool license is a clear violation of the lordship of the Lord Jesus Christ over our church."[12] The center operated without a license from 1981 to 1988, refusing to file compliance reports with the Department of Social Services; in fact, it refused to allow Social Services on its premises to inspect the facility. The center did agree to follow on a "voluntary basis" the requirements for fire, health and safety concerns.

The court recognized the sincerity of the church's belief system, but said that even though the practice of religion was severely burdened by the licensing requirement, the compelling interest standard sustained the requirement. There was no other reasonable way to provide for the welfare and safety of children than to require licensing and inspection for things like the financial stability of the institution, the code compliance for building structure and safety mechanisms, for teacher-student ratios and for program requirements that reflected modern-day theories of good pedagogy and theories of optimal learning environments.

With respect to the discipline issue, the court elicited testimony that illustrated the fact that the school activities were *permitted* by the faith but were not *required* by the faith. This distinction was critical to the court's holding that to sustain a free exercise claim

> [p]laintiffs must demonstrate not only that the subject conduct is religiously permitted, but further that the conduct is religiously mandated or otherwise so central to belief that its prohibition would impose a genuine burden on religious expression.[13]

Corporal punishment was not mandated, so the free exercise issue did not apply.

These cases illustrate an important thing. The compelling state interest test and now the reasonableness standard can be easily used to justify a broad range of government regulation. This may or may not be a bad thing, but the application of the tests rests on a judge's assumption that regulation is legitimate because the activity really is not very religious in nature. The analysis in *North Valley* is the same as the analysis of the district court in *Forest Hills* on remand. However, this approach conflicts with the Supreme Court's perspective of the nature of religious activity in *Amos*. There, the Court said that separating the religious from the secular activity of a church was not within the court's discretion. Here, this separation is done by judges, and it determines the outcome of the case. The courts are ignoring the relationship between faith and the public sphere, ignoring the fact that for many people, faith defines the way children are reared and schooled. Faith defines the pedagogy to be used in schools. Faith is, for many, both private and necessarily public.

In the next section, the Supreme Court faces a similar dilemma and handles it differently than it did in *Amos*.

Funding Private Social Service Agencies

Traditionally, much of the welfare in this country was a private, voluntary action rather than a governmental one. Accordingly, churches and church-related institutions were at the forefront of the "social work" charitable activity in the United States.

The twentieth century brought government involvement into the social service arena, but because the private agency network was so entrenched, most of the government contribution came in the form of aid to agencies already functioning. Because so many of the welfare or charitable agencies had a religious tie, the government opened itself to charges that its financial contribution to religious institutions violated the establishment clause of the First Amendment. The interesting thing is that although the parallel issue of government aid to religious schools spawned a tremendous amount of litigation at state and federal levels, government aid to "religious social welfare" agencies has been litigated with vigor only over the past ten years.

This section of this chapter examines the jurisprudence that defines the limits of government aid to religious social service agencies. Again, what is the difference between a religious organization and a charitable one? Is there a difference between government aid to a church-run soup kitchen and aid given to a soup kitchen run by people who happen to believe that God wants them to help the poor? What about a group that believes it is its moral duty to feed the poor, but has no common faith tying it together? How do courts make this decision, and what are the implications of the courts' distinctions?

At the time of this writing, the U.S. Congress has passed the Charitable Choice provision of the 1996 Welfare bills, and President George W. Bush has demonstrated his commitment to using federal funds to encourage the work of faith-based social service agencies. Although many constitutional scholars believe such partnership is legal, the details of the partnerships become critical in dealing with First Amendment issues. Litigation is likely to follow.

Bowen v Kendrick: Again, A Decade of Conflict

In this case the Supreme Court determined that the government may fund social service agencies with religious ties as long as those agencies are not "pervasively sectarian." However, after ten years of litigation that continues today, answers to the following questions are still uncertain: what does it mean to be pervasively sectarian, and how do institutions get funding to fulfill their charitable mission while still maintaining enough religious identity to claim exemption from state laws that do damage to their belief systems?

Legal analysis of the relationship between government and religious social service agencies became important in 1981 when Congress passed the Adolescent Family Life Act (AFLA). The AFLA was passed by Congress in response to the "severe adverse health, social and economic consequences" that often follow pregnancy and childbirth among unmarried adolescents. It is an act with several purposes:

- to promote self-discipline and other prudent approaches to the problem of adolescent premarital sexual relations;
- to promote adoption as an alternative for adolescent parents;
- to establish new approaches to the delivery of care services for pregnant teenagers;
- to support research concerning social causes and consequences of teenage premarital sexual involvement.

Grant recipients are to provide care services for pregnant teens and to provide prevention services, including

> pregnancy testing, maternity counseling, adoption counseling and referral services, prenatal and postnatal health care, nutritional information, counseling, child care, mental health services, educational services relating to family life and problems associated with adolescent premarital sexual relations.[14]

In creating the AFLA, Congress recognized that certain social problems were so complex that government action alone would be insufficient. Therefore, some problems should be addressed "through a variety of integrated and essential services provided to adolescents and their families by other family members, religious and charitable organizations, voluntary associations, and other groups in the private sector as well as services provided by publicly sponsored initiatives."[15] Congress is recognizing the role that nongovernmental organizations play in the social fabric of our society; it is also recognizing the public sphere role of religious organizations that we often call "private."

Since the passage of the Act, grant money has gone to private and public hospitals, private and public health care agencies, private community centers, private and public educational agencies and charitable organizations. Many of these agencies have formal ties to churches, and many of them consider themselves to be religious whether or not they are formally owned by a church.

In 1984, a lawsuit was filed by a group of taxpayers, the American Jewish Congress, the ACLU and three Methodist ministers claiming that the AFLA was unconstitutional because it violated the establishment clause of the First Amendment.[16] Accordingly, the district court found the AFLA unconstitutional because "religion" was integrated into the goals of the Act and because religious organizations actually received money. Specifically, the court applied the three-part *Lemon* test, concluding that the AFLA had a valid secular purpose which was to "prevent social and economic injury" caused by teenage pregnancy. However, the court said that the AFLA had the direct effect of advancing religion because it expressly required grant applicants to describe how they would involve religious organizations in the provisions of services.

When the case was appealed, the United States Supreme Court found that there was nothing necessarily religious about education or counseling services, even if those services were provided by a sectarian agency. Applying the *Lemon* test, the Court rejected the assumption of the district court that religiously affiliated grantees under the AFLA were unable to fulfill their functions in a secular manner. It agreed with the lower court that because the reduction of social and economic problems was the primary purpose of the Act, the legislative purpose was secular. However, the Supreme Court said that an "impermissible effect" did not exist simply because Congress recognized the role religious organizations play in solving "secular problems." The Court distinguished between institutions that are "pervasively sectarian" and those that are merely religious, saying that only aid to organizations that could not separate their religious teaching from their service was unconstitutional.

The Court also found that the statute's grant monitoring provision did not violate the third prong of *Lemon* because there was no excessive entanglement. The monitoring of AFLA grants is necessary to ensure that public money is to be spent in the way that Congress intended and in a way that comports with the establishment clause. However, said the Court, there is no reason to assume that the religious organizations which may receive AFLA grants are "pervasively sectarian" in the same sense as are, for example, parochial schools.

The Supreme Court was obviously trying to salvage the partnership between government and churches, a partnership that has done great service to citizens of this country with respect to serving the needy. But, the Court's jurisprudence and its definition of religion put it in an untenable position. Separation of church and state that equates "neutrality" and "nonreligious" prohibits church/state partnership. To preserve the partnership the Court had to find a way to define the church activity as nonreligious.

The difficulty presented by the analysis of *Bowen* becomes clear when one examines the litigation that *Bowen* spawned. Three years after the Supreme Court handed down its position on the funding of social service institutions, a group of plaintiffs again represented by Kendrick sued Louis Sullivan, the secretary of the Department of Health and Human Services, for continuing to fund "pervasively sectarian" organizations like A Woman's Choice, Catholic Social Services and so forth.[17]

The *Bowen* lawsuit was reactivated in federal district court with a plea for summary judgment on the issue of the sectarian nature of several organizations. After examining more than 1,750 documents supporting the defendants' claims that their organizations *were religious*, but not *pervasively* so, the court concluded that summary judgment was not appropriate and that the organizations would have to engage in a series of trials to determine the level of sectarian-ness of each.

Although the court did not give specific guidance for the judges who would be presiding over those trials, its approach to the nature of religion is enlightening. The court held that the "pervasively sectarian" standard was a factual issue that could be determined based on the individual situations of each institution separately. It cautioned that judges should limit their trials to whether a grantee's secular purposes and religious mission are inextricably intertwined, emphasizing that it would not be enough to show that the recipient of a challenged grant was affiliated with a religious institution or that it was religiously inspired.

According to the Court, the question is this: is religion so pervasive that a substantial portion of the institution's functions are subsumed in the religious mission? This question is based on an assumption *diametrically opposed* to that of the Court in *Amos*. In *Amos* the justices said we cannot separate the secular from the sectarian or religious acts of a religious institution. In *Bowen* the Court concluded that we must.

The facts surrounding the organizations at issue were disputed, and the evidence that the defendants used to show their lack of "pervasive sectarianism" illustrate the difficult position that judges will be in when they have to make factual rulings.

The plaintiffs argued that the religious missions of the organizations were wrapped up with the dissemination of services that the organizations rendered to their clients. In support of this position they argued that the religious organizations had policies which prohibited deviation from religious doctrine or which required employees to abide by religious principles. Religious leaders were on the Board of Directors of the organizations, and many of the organizations discriminated on the basis of religion in their hiring decisions.

The defendants argued that even if this was true, pervasive sectarianism did not exist because the organizations created separate divisions to carry out the tasks for which they received AFLA funding. These separate divisions provided "secular services" excising any religious references in their literature, and instructing staff to keep "personal convictions (religious, political, prejudiced or social)" to themselves.

How are judges to resolve this dispute? One problem is that the debate over the religious nature of materials used by the sectarian organizations involved discussion about the "religiousness" of phrases like "morality," "values," "religion" and "spirituality." The Supreme Court suggests that institutions can do moral or good deeds, be religiously identified, but still not do those deeds in a religious way. In deciding these cases under the AFLA, will the fact finder have to determine whether there is a moral, value-neutral way for religious organizations to teach about sexuality?

In 1990, a district court in Minnesota compiled a list of factors that members of the Supreme Court had used to determine the "pervasively sectarian" nature of institutions.

1. The institution operates under supervision of a religious order.
2. The employees are members of a religious order, diocese or church.
3. Religious symbols can be found on the institution's premises.
4. Religious instruction occurs.
5. Non-church affiliated students or clients are not required to attend the religious (or moral) instruction.
6. Religion is not required in the "secular" teaching or servicing of clientele.
7. Employees must adhere to a specific set of tenets.
8. Most of the students or clientele are of a particular faith.
9. Preference is given to students or clientele of a particular faith.
10. Governing church elects board of trustees.
11. Governing church has power over financial issues of organization.
12. Governing church can amend the charter of the institution.
13. Handbooks of institutions refer to God, Christianity or faith.
14. The students or clientele are of an impressionable age.
15. The institution subscribes to a statement of principles on academic freedom or freedom of conscience for its employees.
16. Restrictions exist on what employees may advise or teach (and the level at which these restrictions are or are not enforced).
17. The level of institutional autonomy.
18. Whether or not the institution makes a report to an affiliated church.
19. Whether or not church affiliated clergy have a role in the institution.
20. Whether or not church affiliated services are held at the institution.
21. Encouragement of spiritual devotion (is it allowed, or required, or advocated?)
22. Existence of religious indoctrination.
23. Do religious courses or discussion supplement curriculum; if so, are they separated from secular courses?
24. Does prayer exist at the institution?
25. Does talk of theology cover the broad range of human experience or only religion?
26. Are decisions regarding hiring (except in theology courses) made without regard to religion?
27. Can the institution document that it protects clients from proselytizing?
28. Are any required activities presided over by clergy or rabbis? Do they wear clerical garb?[18]

Although the district court cautioned that the list should be used only as a guide, not a litmus test, it is difficult to determine how anyone could make this judgment without saying "nineteen of the factors exist; therefore, the institution is pervasively sectarian."

The *Bowen* cases, ironically, have placed religious institutions in the role of arguing that their instruction is religiously neutral. In *Nelson*, the Minnesota case, even though the catalogs of colleges claimed that "there can be no division between sacred and secular subjects" or "considering education in the light of Christ, there can be no division between sacred and secular subjects," the court found the institutions to be not pervasively sectarian.

It is possible that when the post-*Bowen* cases get back up to the Supreme Court, the Court will separate social service agencies into different categories. This would be disastrous for the state of charitable organizations in this country. Would the Court decide that agencies distributing physical services are not pervasively sectarian, but those distributing advice are?

The *Forest Hills, Amos, Smith,* and *Bowen* cases suggest that religious institutions are between a rock and a hard place:

- The government may grant religious institutions exemptions from laws that other institutions must adhere to, but the government is not bound by the Constitution to do so;
- Without legislative exemption, an institution may adhere to its religious identity, but not if it conflicts with a compelling interest of the state. This rule may be even further limited depending on the development of *Smith*: adhere to your religious identity, but not if it conflicts with a valid, neutral state law of general applicability;
- In order to invoke the above right, the institution must establish that it is truly religious. Prior to *Amos*, this was done by arguing that there was no difference between the secular and religious activity of the institution. Today, the Court recognizes that this separation is almost impossible. This grants extra freedom regarding the regulation issue

But

- If you are a religious institution, you cannot receive government funding unless and until you establish the difference between the secular and the religious activity of your institution.

The main problem here is that the judicial division between *religious* and *secular* that *Amos* stepped away from was reactivated by the Court in *Bowen* with the pervasively sectarian category.

Notes

1. *Forest Hills Early Learning Center v Grace Baptist Church and the State of Virginia*, 487 F.Supp. 1378 (E.D.Va.1979), reversed and remanded, 642 F.2d 448, 540 F.Supp. 1046, affirmed in part, vacated in part and remanded, 728 F.2d 230; 661 F.Supp 300, reversed 846 F.2d 260, 262; rehearing denied, cert. denied 109 S.Ct. 837 (1989). This chapter draws from Julia Stronks, "Social Service Agencies and Religious Freedom" in Stanley Carlson-Thies and James Skillen, *Welfare in America· Christian Perspectives on a Policy in Crisis* (Grand Rapids, Mich.: Eerdmans Publishing Co, 1996), 480-504, and appears here with permission.
2. *Forest Hills*, 301.
3. *Forest Hills*, 309, emphasis added.
4. *Forest Hills*, 303.
5. *Forest Hills*, 303.
6. *Forest Hills*, 311.
7. *Forte v Coler*, 724 F.Supp. 488,490 (M.C.Fla. 1989).
8. *Salvation Army v New Jersey Department of Community Affairs*, 919 F.2d 183 (3rd Cir. 1990).
9. *North Valley Baptist Church v McMahon*, 696 F.Supp 518, 520 (E.D. Cal. 1988).
10. *North Valley*, 520.
11. *North Valley*, 520.
12. *North Valley*, 521.
13. *North Valley*, 531.
14. 42 U.S.C. ss 300z.
15. 42 U.S.C. ss 300z.
16. *Bowen v Kendrick*, 487 U.S. 589 (1988).
17. *Kendrick v Sullivan*, 766 F.Supp. 1180 (D.D.C. 1991).
18. *Minnesota Federation of Teachers v Nelson*, 740 F.Supp. 694 (D. Minn. 1990).

Part Three

What Does It Mean to Be Neutral?

Chapter Six

What Part of Life Is Religious?

When you look at the way that case law has developed, it is clear that there are three primary inconsistencies in the way that judges perceive religious belief. First, some judges say that religion means belief in extratemporal reality; others say religion is any "belief system." Second, some judges believe they can clearly separate religious activity from secular activity; other judges believe that what might look like secular activity becomes religious activity for religious adherents. Finally, some judges believe religion is private and can be kept out of the public arena; others believe that faith necessarily defines public, social activity. Judges' different views of religion result in inconsistent, troublesome jurisprudence.

Many judges believe that religion means church, prayer and belief in a transcendent God. This approach parallels the "subjective" definition of religion used by the Supreme Court in *Reynolds* and *Davis*, prior to the "ultimate meaning" approach articulated in the 1965 *Seeger* case. Protestantism is religion (*Kamehameha).* Proselytizing the Christian faith is religion (*Voswinkel, Baz*). Belief in creation is religion (*McLean*). Baptists are religious (*McCrory*). Ministers and pastors of Christian churches are religious (*Rayburn*).

Not all judges, however, articulate their assumptions about religion very clearly. In many of the decisions, the judges' assumptions are hidden in their statements about what religion is or is not—statements that receive no explanation or clarification because the judges believe that their approach is unanimous. For example, in the *McLean* creation science case, the judge held without discussion that evolution was obviously not a religion. In *Pena*, a belief in eating cat food did not even receive cursory examination as a religion. In *Bellamy*, the judge dismissed the idea that the ritual and ceremony of the KKK could provide a foundation for religious belief. In all of these cases, the judges passed over the argument of those claiming that the belief system was a religion by appealing to the "obvious" and to "common sense."

Contrast these decisions to those of the judges who consciously examine the role that a belief system plays in an adherent's life. In *Africa*, although the judge found that the belief system was not a religion, he went to great lengths to explain that his finding was not based on the fact that the MOVE organization did not believe in God. Rather, MOVE was not a religion because it did not address fundamental and ultimate questions. By focusing on the role that a belief system plays in an adherent's life, judges have found witchcraft and Transcendental Meditation to be religions. Furthermore, in the curriculum cases, this examination played a critical role in determining whether or not public schools established religion by teaching morality or belief systems of any sort. Judge Brevard Hand held that government school teachings of civic morality can constitute a religion that parallels the belief system of conservative Christians.

However, the definition of religion involves more than the categorizing of belief systems. Judges do not very often face either the circumstances presented to them in the Kozy Kitten Cat Food case or the argument that the KKK is a church. Most of the decisions that judges make involve consideration of what is and what is not religious *activity*. Some judges think religious activity can be easily separated from secular activity. On the other hand, for some judges, the distinction is not so clear.

This is the debate that defines the conflict in the employment cases and in the social service cases. Child care, education of children, profit-making business and janitorial work seem to be clearly secular endeavors to some judges, even when they are performed by people who perceive the acts to be religious (*Townley, Forest Hills, Pacific Press, Wessling*, lower court in *Amos*). Therefore, government regulation of these acts is found to be legitimate.

However, other judges recognize that for some faiths, the belief system defines all activity. So, secretarial work, raising and educating children and janitorial work are just as much religious activity as is church attendance (dissent in *Townley*, majority opinion of Supreme Court in *Amos, Salvation Army, Forest Hills* appellate court decision). Government may not regulate these activities unless it establishes that the regulation is compelled by concern for something important like the safety of citizens.

Just what is the problem here? First, there is incoherence in the definition of religion which means that different judges' personal views about religion will determine the outcome of the case. Second, depending on your definition of religion, the government can be accused of imposing a faith on groups in society by refusing to recognize that the belief system that supports government policies parallels the role that religion plays in peoples' lives. Only secular subjects get taught in schools, and only non-pervasively sectarian social service agencies get government funding. However, "secular" seems to mean "nonreligious" and therefore, the definition of religion is critical. If religion is that which involves God, then, in some cases, government is advancing belief systems that reject God at the expense of those that accept God. In other cases, by exempting churches and other religious institutions from employment discrimination law, government arguably favors belief systems that accept God.

On the other hand, if religion means the same as "belief system," then as government regulates curriculum, employment and the structure of discipline at church-related day care centers, it imposes a set of belief systems which is the equivalent of imposing religion.

At the root of these problems is the inherent conflict between an *idea* and a *reality*: an idea that if something is religious it ought to be beyond the reach of any government control—government must keep its hands off the inner heart and direction of life, and the *reality* that religious things are not simply inner realities but have a social presence.[1]

Generally, in our country, we do acknowledge that government must pay attention to that social side, but some judges do this by concluding that government regulation is legitimate *because the public realm is secular.* This creates a problem when the inner heart directs public, social action. Government regulation might well be needed, but judges walk into a trap when they say government may not regulate religion, but government may regulate the public. This forces them to conclude that religion is private. Then, when religion directs public life, they have no way to articulate a rule for legitimate government regulation. They apply the compelling interest test, but this test is applied from the prior assumption that religion is private. Economics, caring for children, writing newspapers, making profit—these are of the public, secular realm (*Pacific Press, Townley, Forest Hills, Salvation Army*). The compelling interest test is designed to answer the question: how do we regulate faith when it affects the public realm? But, we beg the question. We have already decided that many things, because they are public, are secular.

The problem is not just in the judges, but involves the assumptions that we all make about faith, and its role in both society and the lives of individuals. At times the courts, churches and faith-based organizations other than churches have *all* argued that religion is an "added" quality or activity, and that institutions shaped by religion are uniquely moral, whereas other institutions are neutral or value free. Therefore, government should keep its hands off these religious institutions. But, this "hands off" approach has problems of its own. Why should the curricular choices and disciplining practices of a Christian daycare or school be singled out for special control or for special exemption from regulation? What is it about religious faith that separates it from other worldviews? What separates religious activity from activity that is directed by other "inner realities?"

The free exercise clause and the establishment clause of the First Amendment assume an understanding of what religion is, but our jurisprudence illustrates that there is anything but agreement on the definition of religion or religious activity. The cases discussed in this book illustrate that before we can apply the First Amendment, we must consider more carefully the issue of definitions. What is religion? Moreover, a solution to the religion problem does not rest in merely choosing a definition of religion. To solve the conflicts reflected in the employment cases, the social service cases and the curriculum cases, a solution must include consideration of what is and what is not religious activity. And, it must include consideration of the relationship between faith and the rest of life.

Scholars' Solutions

First Amendment jurisprudence has been in flux and criticized severely for decades. Interestingly, however, little of the debate has centered around the definition of religion. Most of the criticism falls into one of two categories: explanation as to why one of the two religion clauses in the First Amendment should take precedence over the other, or explanation as to how a particular value like "neutrality" or "religious freedom" or "separation between church and state" should influence case law.

This section examines these criticisms in light of the definitional problems discussed so far. Do the scholars' solutions to the "religion" problem solve the definition questions?

Chapter two illustrated the Supreme Court's application of both the accommodationist stance and the separationist approach at different points in history. This application has involved the development of different tests to be applied to cases: the compelling interest test developed for application of the free exercise clause, and the much criticized three-prong secular purpose test developed for application of the establishment clause. The problem is that both tests assume that we have an understanding of what "religion" is. Neither approach grapples with the definitional problems. The broad definition of religion applied in accordance with free exercise cases fails to distinguish between religion and other viewpoints; however, the separationist establishment clause cases fail to assert a consistent difference between a secular state interest and a religious interest.

The confusion created by these different approaches has led scholars to criticize the clauses and the tests applied. Even the judges join in the criticism. The *Smith* Court exhibited a clear step away from the compelling interest test, and six members of the current Court have stated that they are unsatisfied with the *Lemon* test. Both Justice Kennedy and Justice O'Connor have offered substitutes. Kennedy suggests that the *Lemon* test be replaced with a "deference standard." The government should be forbidden to coerce people into accepting religious belief or acting in religious ways, and the government should be forbidden to proselytize. O'Connor suggests that the proper test ought to focus on prohibiting government from "endorsing" religion. The problem is, however, that even these new tests assume an understanding of what religion is before they can be applied.

The irony is that the First Amendment language appears to compel courts to distinguish between religions and philosophies, but the very act of distinguishing the difference requires a definition of religion and involves the Court in determining religious orthodoxy.[2] The problem with defining religion rests on the purpose of the religion clauses themselves—defining religion will limit the protection of religion to those beliefs that the judges deem to be real. Therefore, some of the scholars who have addressed the definitional problem solve it by coming up with ways to apply the First Amendment while avoiding the need to define the term. Others believe that they have a definition that is "true religion."

Judges are using inconsistent approaches to the concept of religion, but scholars have not spent much time giving guidance in this area of the law. In the literature that does consider definitions of religion, most scholars have been content to advocate for either the *Davis* approach or the *Seeger* approach.

Scholars that align with the *Davis* argument say that a content-based approach to religion should be used: "this is religion, that is not." Unfortunately, there is little agreement about what criteria should be used. Depending on their own theological or sociological background, scholars like law professor Stephen Carter, Judge John Noonan, Mircea Eliade and others have advocated definitions highlighting one of the following elements:

- some focus on God or a Supreme Being
- others focus on definitions that emphasize an ethical system
- others focus on worship or communal experience
- others focus on beliefs that arguably hold extratemporal consequences for the adherent

Most scholars who argue on behalf of a substantive definition of religion say that it is necessary in order to restrict the beliefs that qualify for protection under the First Amendment. They argue that for beliefs to be protected, the violation of those beliefs must hold extratemporal consequences for the adherent.

Law professor Stanley Ingber criticizes this approach, saying that it is underinclusive in that it excludes nonwestern faiths. However, he gives some historical context when he explains that the foundation of a substantive definition of religion is set in the desire to protect the Constitution. Ideology, or general belief systems, should not receive as much protection as religion because "if the Constitution is to have any significance, all conflicting ideologies must defer to it and to those laws promulgated according to its mandates."[3] Religious conscience is different from ideology and receives special protection because the First Amendment asserts this one concession for pre-Enlightenment belief. The Enlightenment embodied individualistic liberalism. Those who live under the Constitution abide by individualistic precepts; however, those who answer to a higher, transcendent order face different obligations. "The obligations imposed by religion are of a different, high nature than those derived from human relationships . . . they are not part of the agenda of public debate."[4] So, to receive accommodation of your faith, you must show that you have an inconsistent duty that is imposed on you from a higher or divine source.

All of these substantive criteria have troublesome aspects. First, they each leave out a worldview that is clearly recognized as religious both by our culture and by the courts. When you look at beliefs that are recognized as religious (Hinduism, Buddhism, Christianity, Judaism, Islam, Wicca, Shintoism and so forth) you cannot put together a list of elements that are common to all.[5] Second, even if we could agree on which substantive definition to use our struggle would not be solved. We still have not addressed the nature of religious activity or the implications of religion for the rest of life. Third, substantive definitions of religion counteract the purpose of the religion clauses themselves—defining religion will limit the protection of religion to those beliefs that the judges deem to be real.

So, some scholars who have addressed the definitional problem solve it by coming up with ways to apply the First Amendment while avoiding the need to define the term. They use a functional approach: "this functions similarly to religion, so treat it as religion."

One functional approach to religion that receives much attention derives from the "ultimate concern" test used in the *Seeger* case.[6] This definition explicates the judges' perspective in *Seeger* by suggesting that the core value underlying the free exercise clause is the inviolability of conscience. Therefore, with respect to the free exercise clause only, ultimate concerns should be the defining criteria. Ultimate concerns are those acts

> of the total personality, not a movement of a special and discrete part of the total being . . . the single most important interest in [an individual's] life . . . the free exercise clause demands that any concern deemed to be ultimate be protected, regardless of how 'secular' that concern might seem to be.[7]

This Harvard Law Review Note points out that ultimate concerns cannot be superseded, and adherents must be willing to disregard self-interest and to accept martyrdom in preference to violating the beliefs.

This strength of this definition is that it seems to be fairly flexible; it can encompass nontraditional religions. However, its standards are so strict that it would exclude many people who claim to be religious but are not articulate at identifying their fundamental ultimate concerns.[8] Stanley Ingber criticizes the definition as being so demanding that it protects a limited few and also so broad that it leaves no distinction between religion and any other value system; thus, it becomes meaningless. How many people are conscious of their one true belief? How many of us are willing to martyr ourselves? He argues that the definition also discriminates against people who do not have one ultimate concern, but who do live a life committed to a set of fundamental principles.

Others have used the same approach articulated by the Harvard Note, but expand the test to include "cardinal concerns." John Mansfield says that religion at its foundational level must provide answers to the ultimate questions of life: human existence, the origin of being, the meaning of suffering and death and the existence of a spiritual reality.[9] But, how do you identify the most important questions? Must belief systems answer all of them or just some of them to qualify as religious? Even if religions always possess underlying theories about human nature or humanity's place in the world, so do other "moral" beliefs. Are these also religious?

Occasionally scholars argue for a two-pronged or bifurcated definition of religion: a functional definition for free exercise cases; a substantive definition for establishment clause cases or vice versa. In free exercise cases, for example, religion could be self-defining. Any adherent who claimed to be religious could be considered religious. Any activity that the adherent claimed to be religious activity would be accepted as religious activity. The compelling interest test would, presumably, be the only limit on religious freedom. The need for a court-accepted definition is eliminated, but is it possible for religion to be a self-defining entity?

Critics argue that two problems arise.[10] First, in free exercise cases, application for exemption from general laws would probably increase exponentially. Anyone with a disagreement over tax policy, criminal law and so forth could argue that his or her beliefs were faith-based. Justice Antonin Scalia has argued that the fabric of government would come unraveled if generally applicable laws with incidental effect on religious exercise were deemed to be presumptively unconstitutional.

Second, if the self-defining principle were invoked, judges could still assess the sincerity of a belief. Judges are more likely to accept the sincerity of a belief if they find that belief to be reasonable.

A final problem with the bifurcated definition is that in establishment clause cases, a substantive definition of religion still results in government's imposition of a set of beliefs on a religious group. Government policies are not neutral in their effect on groups. They also are not neutral in substance. A substantive definition of religion for establishment clause cases fails to solve the curriculum cases or the tension between the funding and regulation of faith-based groups. Many will still argue that government's regulations about employment discrimination, day care discipline policies and public school curricula are faith-based themselves. Furthermore, funding the sectarian institutions but not the pervasively sectarian institutions requires yet another level of definitions.

Adherents of traditional religions will, ironically, lose out under this scheme. Faiths that are unquestionably religious will be free from government interference and will not receive government support. Those that are unquestionably nonreligious will receive government money but will be subject to government regulation. But, those that are arguably religious and arguably nonreligious could be considered religious for free exercise purposes but nonreligious for establishment clause purposes. They will be free from government regulation, and they would also receive government support.[11]

Bifurcated definitions would result in inequity from the perspective of many groups and they fail to help us think through the relationship between law and faith. To say that *religious* is defined in one way for part of the First Amendment and in a different way for another part of the First Amendment leads to an incoherent and inconsistent approach to Constitutional jurisprudence.

However, to argue that religion should be treated differently in different sorts of cases holds more theoretical sway. The problem is that the cases demand an understanding not just of the definition of religion but also of the relationship between religion and the rest of life, and the difference between religious and secular activity. The definitional problems must be dealt with.

A final, proposed solution to the definition problem rests in "reasoning by analogy." This approach suggests that not all belief systems are religious. However, courts can not define religion. So, let belief systems receive the label "religious" if they can show that they align with the factors that have historically and traditionally been considered religious. Kent Greenawalt and George Freeman are the advocates of this perspective. In their analyses of the definition problem, they come, separately, to the same conclusion.[12]

Freeman points out that Eastern and Western religions have common features; these common features should be the starting point for the determination of the "religiousity" of a belief system:

1. A belief in a Supreme Being
2. A belief in a transcendent reality
3. A moral code
4. A world view that provides an account of man's role in the universe and around which an individual organizes his life
5. Sacred rituals and holy days
6. Worship and prayer
7. A sacred text or scripture
8. Membership in a social organization that promotes a religious belief system.

These features are not necessary or sufficient, standing alone. But, in totality, the list describes a paradigm for religion. A paradigm for irreligion is developed by turning each factor on its head: no belief in morality, no rituals, and so forth.

Freeman applies the paradigms by asking: does the government support of an activity promote a paradigmatic religious belief system? If so, the support is unconstitutional. If government support promotes a belief system that is the opposite of the paradigm, then the support is irreligious and is also unconstitutional. However, if the government support is just as likely to promote either type of belief system, it is nonreligious and is constitutional.

Freeman and Greenawalt propose a pluralistic solution that focuses not on a person's activity that may be "religious" or "secular" but rather on the *government* action. Law professor Michael McConnell has suggested that part of our religious freedom jurisprudence must be directed in this fashion, forcing the government to examine its activity. Government should ask not "will this advance religion?" Rather, government should ask "will this advance pluralism? Will government action suppress expression of religious differences?"

Law professor MaryAnn Glendon agrees with McConnell, saying that the major interpretive challenge for the future "will be to accord as much scope as possible to the constitutional guarantee of free exercise in its personal, associational and institutional dimensions while respecting the freedom of conscience of nonbelievers and without preferring one religion to another."[13] Glendon and McConnell believe that society is made up of a variety of social activities like education, government, economics, family and so forth. In this society people and groups approach life from different worldviews. Government, in acting on its responsibilities, must respect the different worldviews that are reflected by the people and institutions that make up society. Government must not take sides between the religious and the secular perspectives but must provide equal justice for all of them.

This approach is very important because it puts us on the path to a new way of handling First Amendment cases.

Are All Perspectives Grounded in Religion?

Emile Durkheim was a French sociologist writing in the late nineteenth and early twentieth century. One of his most important works is *The Elementary Forms of Religious Life* in which he applied methods of natural science to the cross-cultural study of religion.[14] After examining different religions across cultures and back through time to primitive society, Durkheim built on one of his earlier pieces "Concerning the Definition of Religious Phenomena" to conclude that a religion "is a unified system of beliefs and practices relative to sacred things, that is to say, things set apart and forbidden—beliefs and practices which unite into one single moral community called a Church, all those who adhere to it."[15] This definition is a substantive definition that doesn't really differ in detail from the substantive definitions of other scholars. However, Durkheim's real contribution to the question "what is religion" rests in the process he took to achieve his definition.

First, Durkheim insisted that scholars work to rid themselves of prejudicial definitions of religion which are formed primarily by our own experiences. Then, he said, known religious systems should be examined to determine which elements they have in common. That process would result in a non-prejudicial definition of religion.

At the time that Durkheim was writing, religion was generally thought of as both mysterious and based on God or godlike entities. This, to Durkheim, was not a satisfactory perspective on religion because, as he pointed out, there have been many eras when a sense of the mysterious was not a part of religious life. Durkheim pointed to the scholastic period and the seventeenth century as examples. Furthermore, the emphasis on gods failed to account for several different "great religions" that did not emphasize gods, like Buddhism, Jainism, Brahminism and so forth. After his study, Durkheim concluded that all known religious beliefs present one common characteristic: they presuppose a "classification of all the things, real and ideal, of which men think, into two classes or opposed groups, generally designated by two distinct terms which are translated well enough by the words profane and sacred."[16]

At the time magic was a phenomenon that was of great interest to people in general, and of great concern to people that identified themselves as religious. Magic included rites and beings that could be confused with religion under Durkheim's definition and this was troubling to him. Durkheim then expanded on his definition of religion, differentiating it from magic by arguing that religion was public, social and concerned with exploring the good, while magic was private, selfish and potentially harmful. Religion, then, had to involve a group of people that had in common an adherence to a way of life. Magic did not count because in magic were no "lasting bonds which make them members of the same moral community, comparable to that formed by the believers in the same god or the observers of the same cult."[17]

Durkheim's approach to the definition of religion is significant because it lays the foundation for asking questions about the implication of belief systems whether or not they are founded on a Supreme Being. Using Durkheim's approach, one scholar, philosopher Roy Clouser, has developed an argument that takes seriously the difficulties inherent in examining the difference between and among faith, belief and philosophical or moral approaches to life. He argues that *all* worldviews are regulated by religious belief of some type.

> I will contend that one religious belief or another controls theory-making in such a way that the contents of the theories differ depending on the contents of the religious belief they presuppose. In fact, so extensive is this religious influence that virtually all the major disagreements between competing theories in the sciences and in philosophy can ultimately be traced back to differences in their religious presuppositions.
>
> This means that theories about math and physics, sociology and economics, art and ethics, politics and law can never be religiously neutral. They are all regulated by some religious belief. The effects of religious beliefs therefore extend far beyond providing the hope for life after death or influencing moral values and judgments. By con-

> trolling theory-making, they produce important differences in the interpretation of issues that range over the whole of life.[18]

Clouser's argument evolves from his exploration of the nature of religion. He begins by looking at all belief systems that are uncontroversial in their claim to be "religious" and asks what common elements they (and only they) share. His first step was to compile a "short list" of religions including Judaism, Christianity, Islam, Hinduism, Buddhism, Taoism, Egyptian polytheism, Epicureanism, belief in and worship of Ba'al, Druidism, beliefs and worship centered on Isis and Mithra, Zoroastrianism, Shintoism, belief in the Greek gods and so forth. Then, he tried to apply the most widely accepted definitions of religion to the list.

- *Religion as an ethical code*: Shintoism does not have an ethical code, Epicureanism made no connection between belief in gods and duties to humans. Furthermore, Boy Scouts have a moral code but they are not a religion so this category is not helpful.
- *Religion must include worship*: Hindus and Buddhists do not worship.
- *Religion must include a Supreme Being:* Brahman-Atman, the divine concept in Hinduism is not a Supreme Being but rather is being-ness in all individuals. Buddhism says the divine is in nonbeing or Nothingness.
- *Religion must include an Ultimate Concern*: Clouser says that if you look at arguments about Ultimate Concern they are really arguments for one ultimate concern over others—they do not allow for ultimate concerns which are false as well as those which are true. Clouser argues that the practical application of Tillich's perspective, for example, (the one relied on in *Seeger)* rejects many beliefs that our culture easily accepts as religious.

Next, Clouser asked what all the beliefs on the list had in common. He concluded that there was only one thing: each belief accepts something as a form of the divine. Different religious traditions disagree about the *nature* of the divine, but they all center around a *concept* of divinity.

> All religious traditions seem to center around whatever they believe to be divine, but they disagree widely on how that is to be thought of. It is variously believed to be one supreme creator, two ever-opposing forces, a realm populated by many gods, being-itself, nothingness etc.[19]

Clouser proposes that if we are to be clear about what is and what is not religious, we have to distinguish between the *status* of divinity and what is believed to *occupy* that status. If we do that, then we see that all beliefs that we accept as "religious" have in common the fact that they all believe in something as divine or self-existent: something on which all else depends.

This is the key that distinguishes Clouser's approach to religion. If a person's approach to business emerges from her belief in God, that seems religious. But, Clouser argues, if a person's approach to business emerges from the belief that the individual is self-existent—that on which all else depends—that approach is also religious in the broad sense.

> This is true, for example, of the Tao in Taoism, of Yahweh in Judaism and Christianity (Allah in Islam), of Brahman-Atman in Hinduism, and of the Dharmakaya, Void, Nirvana, or Suchness in various branches of Buddhism. And it is also true of the divinities of all the other traditions mentioned on our short list In fact, I have not yet found any religion, whether on or off the short list, which does not explicitly or implicitly share this same idea of the status of divinity. They all believe that the divine is whatever is "just there." And that all that is not divine depends on the divine in the sense that the divine can exist without the nondivine, but the nondivine cannot exist without the divine.[20]

Whatever is believed to be "self-existent" is divine. Clouser explains that for ancient Pythagoreans it was numbers; for Plato, Forms are self-existent; for Jews, Christians, and Muslims, God or Allah is self-existent. And, for many Americans, the individual is believed to be self-existent—that on which all else depends.

If you use the concept of "self-existence" as your foundation for religious belief, it is then possible that all people are "innately religious." If being religious means worshipping God or believing in a Savior, clearly not all are religious. But, if being religious means replacing the concept of God with something else—something that is believed to be the "nondependent reality on which all else depends,"[21] then it is not clear that some are religious and others are not. Not only is every person religious, but every belief becomes religious. "A belief is a religious belief provided that it is a belief in something or other as divine or it is a belief concerning how humans come to stand in proper relation to the divine."[22]

Clouser says that there is nothing inherently religious about eating bread and wine or ringing bells or circumcising babies; rather, these things become religious because of what people believe about the relationship between doing these things and attaining proper relation to the divine.

> A religious belief is any belief in something or other as divine. Divine means having the status of not depending on anything else . . . the materialist who regards physical matter as self-existent and all else as dependent on it will surely not be induced by that belief to pray to subatomic particles or sing hymns to force fields. Nor will a modern rationalist who regards, say, mathematical ways as self-existent be inclined to develop a liturgy of Quantitative Adoration for their worship. Nevertheless, these beliefs ascribe to matter or mathe-

> matical laws, respectively, the same nondependent status that a Jew or Christian accords to Yahweh, or a Hindu attributes to Brahman-Atman. Rather than having no religion at all these people simply have a different idea of what is divine, an idea in which worship is not appropriate.[23]

After examining many different beliefs, Clouser determined that all beliefs can be categorized with respect to "how the nondivine depends on the divine—or a religious dependency arrangement."[24] He found three broad categories of belief and he gives these beliefs the labels Pagan, Biblical or Pantheistic.

In Pagan beliefs the divine is some part of the created universe. For example, although Marx himself was an atheist, Clouser explains that Marx's theories presuppose the self-existence of matter—matter depends on nothing and reality is identical to or dependent on matter. So, Clouser characterizes Marx's beliefs as religious. Clouser includes most concepts of humanism or secular humanism in this category because these beliefs take something about creation to be the "self-existent segment of reality on which all else depends."[25] For Clouser, atheism or secularism are not nonreligious, but rather alternative religious beliefs.

In Pantheistic beliefs, like Hinduism and Buddhism, the divine is not a subdivision of reality, but the nondivine is a subdivision of the divine. There is a continuous reality between the divine and the nondivine, as with the Pagan adherents, but the relationship between them is different.

In Biblical-type beliefs this continuous reality is denied. The Hebrew idea of creation holds that Yahweh (Allah for Islam) is the Creator and is distinct from the universe. The divine brought the nondivine into being—brought the nondivine into existence out of nothing. There is a "fundamental discontinuity between the creator and all else which is his creation."[26]

Clouser explains that beliefs differ on what is divine, and they differ on how the divine relates to what is not divine—and these differences *are not reconcilable.* If we have competing beliefs, government has to either pick one or it has to treat all equally. Under Clouser's perspective true government neutrality toward religion requires an equal, pluralistic approach to all belief systems. The next section explores the recent work of the U.S. Supreme Court Justices who demonstrate some sensitivity to Clouser's approach. The next chapter explores what Clouser's approach would mean to the public policy—what it would look like in the cases of employment law, curriculum debate and government funding of social service institutions.

Clouser's Approach and Recent School Funding Cases

Beginning in the 1990s, Justices Thomas, Rehnquist and Scalia demonstrated their interest in interpreting the religion clauses of the First Amendment in a way that allowed faith to be welcomed into the public square. However, in *Smith* they clearly stated that when the majority believes that it is desirable to limit actions that may be religious actions to an adherent, the majority should be able to do this—it is simply part of the political process that minority religions will lose out. Justice Kennedy usually sides with Thomas, Rehnquist and Scalia. Most of the other justices prefer to decide religious freedom cases in a more traditional way. However, Justice Sandra Day O'Connor has emerged as an important voice in this debate because she often provides a swing vote needed for the success of one side or the other.

O'Connor's concurrence in the December 2000 case *Mitchell v Helms* provided the fifth vote necessary to uphold Chapter 2 of the 1981 Federal Education Consolidation and Improvement Act. However, although she concurred in the result of the plurality opinion, O'Connor went to great lengths to reject the rationale of Justices Thomas, Rehnquist, Scalia and Kennedy. O'Connor's concurrence was based on her earlier assessment of the proper relationship between government funding and faith-based schools articulated in the 1997 case *Agostini v Felton*. Her arguments illuminate some significant issues that the Court will have to deal with as a developing "neutrality toward belief systems" in establishment clause cases bumps up against the special protection that religious belief usually receives in free exercise cases.

To understand the significance of O'Connor's role in *Mitchell*, one has to understand her technique of using "accommodationism" of both behavior and jurisprudence to influence the Court. This part of the chapter first explores O'Connor's background as a tool to understand her role in developing religious freedom jurisprudence. Then, it considers her approach to neutrality toward religion, highlighting the relationship between *Agostini* and *Mitchell*. Finally, it illustrates once again that the Court has to pay more attention to the assumptions it makes about the nature of secular and religious belief.

Justice O'Connor as a Judge

Sandra Day O'Connor was appointed to the Supreme Court in 1981 by President Ronald Reagan. Early studies of O'Connor stressed the fact that she was the first woman on the Supreme Court, attempting to understand her position on feminist issues. But, because O'Connor was not interested in the argument that women speak with a "different voice" than do men, feminist assessments of her work concluded that O'Connor was not a particularly effective jurist. This assessment was furthered by frustration on the part of conservatives because O'Connor could not be relied on to consistently develop what many thought was her conservative perspective.

O'Connor has been called unsophisticated and nonacademic in her approach, but judicial process scholar Nancy Maveety suggests that many have missed O'Connor's very careful jurisprudential strategy. According to Maveety, O'Connor's pragmatic legal reasoning has made an important contribution to the developing conservatism of the Court. O'Connor's primary contribution to the Court is her "accommodationist strategy" in both behavior and jurisprudence.

> O'Connor's doctrinal policies are nonformulaic, they encourage only modest, incremental change and thus have broad appeal to the various moderates and moderate conservatives on the Court and can serve as the agents of compromise in contentious legal areas. For O'Connor, jurisprudential flexibility is both a philosophy of judging and a strategy for collective bargaining.[27]

Jurisprudential accommodationism involves rejecting "bright line" analysis, focusing, instead, on a balancing approach. Maveety explains that O'Connor is flexible, contextual and fact specific in her legal reasoning. She is hesitant to overturn precedent, and she reasons by exception. She is less ideological than other conservatives and more sensitive to the history of specific factual situations.

Behavioral accommodationism involves a strategic approach that includes swing voting, the writing of separate opinions and the development of varying coalitional alliances.[28] O'Connor has said that her attempt to balance interests and her commitment to coalition bargaining stems from her legislative branch experience. Maveety's study demonstrates that O'Connor's coalitional alliance swings back and forth between her conservative and liberal colleagues across issues over past decades, most specifically in the areas of civil rights, church-state relations and abortion.

O'Connor's effort to bridge the perspective of different voices on the Court can be seen in her concurring opinions. More than half her opinions in church-state areas are clarifying concurrences developing her effort to replace the much-maligned three-part *Lemon* test in establishment cases with an "endorsement test."

The endorsement test reflects O'Connor's perspective on neutrality theory. She advocates what I will refer to as "worldview neutrality": government should not benefit or discriminate against people on the basis of their worldview. In establishment clause cases this means that religious worldviews should not be endorsed, advocated nor discriminated against. And, in free exercise cases people should not have to give up their place as citizens just because of their religious worldview—subject to the compelling interest test.

In both free exercise cases and establishment cases O'Connor exhibits a balancing approach arguing that government should neither endorse nor disapprove of religion. For her, the context of government relations with religious activity is significant. What is interesting about her approach, however, is that her concern for worldview pluralism sometimes conflicts with what seems to be an assumption that government support of secular belief is also a reflection of appropriate neutrality. It is this switching back and forth between "government neutrality between and among worldviews" and "government neutrality occurs when secular belief is supported" that makes O'Connor confusing. Her bifurcated approach to neutrality builds bridges between the two wings of the Court, but it also frustrates those who follow developing neutrality theory.

O'Connor Over Time

O'Connor's first criticism of *Lemon* came in a concurrence in 1984. *Lynch v Donnelly* upheld a Christian crèche on city property. The *Lemon* test applied by the majority had asked:

- Did the action have a secular purpose--did legislators have a nonreligious, secular purpose in mind or were they motivated by religious, sectarian goals?
- Was religion advanced or inhibited?
- Was government excessively entangled with religion?

O'Connor's concurring opinion, however, asked: did the government action convey an endorsement of or a disapproval of religion?

In *Lynch*, Chief Justice Burger and dissenter Justice Brennan were debating whether the Court should reject *Lemon* for a more contextual and historical analysis of church/state interaction.[29] When O'Connor concurred, she drew from both opinions to argue that the crèche's physical setting among nonreligious artifacts and the cultural response to the religious dimension of Christmas should be taken into account to conclude that religion was not endorsed nor disapproved of in this pluralistic display. Here you see worldview pluralism demonstrated. Government should not be hostile to religious belief—thus, the crèche can be a part of a display. But, government should not endorse religion over other belief systems—thus, it is important that the crèche be included among other worldview or philosophic symbols.

In the 1989 *Allegheny* case Justice Blackmun used O'Connor's contextual approach of the endorsement test to invalidate a nativity scene standing alone and to uphold a display that combined several secular and faith-related symbols. O'Connor concurred, again using a separate opinion to comment on Blackmun's analysis and to defend the endorsement test against the dissents of Kennedy, Rehnquist, Scalia and White. Although O'Connor's endorsement test had by this time been used by numerous judges in establishment clause cases, it was also criticized by Justice Anthony Kennedy—not only because he prefers an approach that tests only for government coercion, but because he objected to the role that a mere concurring opinion had played in developing court doctrine. Kennedy failed to give O'Connor credit for the work she had done to integrate the concerns of both wings of the Court. O'Connor agreed with the conservative branch that coercive proselytizing was unconstitutional but she assuaged the liberal branch by arguing that subtle favoritism toward religion was also unconstitutional.

Maveety points out that by 1992 establishment cases were no longer referencing the *Lemon* test. This rejection of *Lemon* without a specific overturning of the case was made possible, in part, by O'Connor's approach.

> O'Connor's idiosyncratic but successful sponsorship of the endorsement test attests to a particular kind of quiet doctrinal leadership. Her assertion of a new approach to establishment clause problems has been subdued, both in method (the concurring opinion) and content (reconciling her test with the *Lemon* inquiry). Her success has also been somewhat subdued: no majority has repudiated *Lemon* and embraced the endorsement test in its stead. O'Connor has nevertheless been the agent of creative compromise for a fragile but controlling coalition in this area of church-state jurisprudence.[30]

In the early 1990s O'Connor began to expand the endorsement test to cover an integrated philosophy of church/state relations in both establishment and free exercise cases. In *Lee v Weisman* invalidating the use of prayer in graduation ceremonies and in *Lamb's Chapel* involving after-hours use of public school property by faith-based organizations, the endorsement test was employed to demonstrate that a "message of exclusion" was a primary principle for religious freedom jurisprudence. This connects O'Connor's establishment clause concerns with her free exercise concerns.

In free exercise cases, O'Connor holds fast to the notion that religious belief deserves protection not available to other beliefs, insisting that the strict scrutiny test be applied when evaluating laws that do not target a religion but nonetheless have an impact on limiting a person's religious activity. A person's civic role in civil society should not be diminished in any way just because that person acts on his or her religious beliefs. O'Connor believes this to be true unless and until the government demonstrates that it can pass the strict scrutiny test. If the government has a compelling interest in limiting a person's religious activity, and if the government takes the least restrictive alternative to achieving its compelling interest, the limit on religious activity will stand. O'Connor places this bar high and it is not easy for the government to pass this test. However, it is significant that for O'Connor this protection extends only to activity that stems from religious belief—not from any worldview belief. Here, worldview neutrality is compromised, but it seems to have happened in an unintentional way.

In the mid-1980s the conservative wing of the Court was beginning to assess free exercise cases without clear reference to the compelling interest test. This foreshadowed their 1990 rejection of the compelling interest test for cases involving laws that were on their face neutral toward religion.[31] As early as 1986 O'Connor had begun to express concern about this. In both *Roy* and *Goldman* she wrote separate opinions explicitly applying the compelling interest test and assessing whether or not the state had used the least restrictive means available to achieve its interest. She frustrated the conservative wing by her insistence on the use of the test and disappointed the liberal wing in *Roy* by finding that the test had been met, upholding the government's requirement of social security numbers even in the face of religious objection.

The critical decision for O'Connor's free exercise approach is *Lyng*, which involved a U.S. Forest Service road paved through national forest lands used for Native American spiritual ceremonies. Maveety points out that it is key because O'Connor's opinion for the Court used a *coercion* test, Kennedy's test, for free exercise cases rather than the compelling interest test. O'Connor said that the coercion test was appropriate when otherwise neutral and lawful government programs had only "incidental effects" on religious practices. But, because her opinion was so contextualized and fact-specific, the discussion about incidental effects was confusing to the developing free exercise jurisprudence. The liberal branch of the Court felt betrayed by O'Connor and the conservative branch used her *Lyng* analysis, over her objections, to lay the foundation for their scuttling of the compelling interest test in *Smith*. Maveety argues that O'Connor's behavioral accommodationism can be seen here because her "linguistic maneuverings" demonstrate her willingness to give up some doctrine in order to write the opinion for the Court. Unfortunately, in *Lyng* her judicial accommodationism produced a "doctrinal lurch that was not consensus building in the long run."[32] It is unclear, though, whether O'Connor's position in *Lyng* was a self-conscious departure from her own approach.

Two years later Justice Scalia used *Lyng* to argue in *Smith* that strict scrutiny was no longer necessary for free exercise cases that involved laws that did not, on their face, target religion. O'Connor concurred in judgment but emphasized that the Court could not reject its accepted free exercise approach—rather, it should affirm the necessity of using the strict scrutiny test. In her view government should not make abandonment of religion the price of an equal place in the community of citizens. She said that even neutral laws could coerce a person to violate religious duties and she was hostile to the conservative wing's assertion that all beliefs should be subject to the political will of the majority as long as government refrained from specifically targeting religion in its statutes.

The confusion developing in free exercise cases is seen in the diverse approaches to a unanimous agreement to overturn a Hialeah, Florida, city ordinance banning ritual sacrifice of animals.[33] Kennedy wrote the opinion that said, like in *Smith*, neutral laws of general applicability need no compelling justification on the part of the government. But, almost all of the judges wrote separate opinions clarifying their approach to the uprooted free exercise doctrine. O'Connor took another opportunity to assert her defense of the strict scrutiny test but over the following ten years the Court has never firmly returned to this doctrine in cases where religion is not specifically targeted by statutes.

The problem is that for O'Connor the logical extension of the worldview neutrality she based her endorsement test on in establishment cases means that religion should not get special treatment in free exercise cases. Justices Scalia,

Rehnquist, Thomas and even Kennedy demonstrated in *Smith* that they were prepared to accept that. O'Connor is not. The logical extension of a worldview neutrality position in establishment cases involving financing of institutions means that government ought to financially support a variety of worldviews, including those that are religious. Although the members of the Court seem flexible on this point as it relates to social service institutions, they have been less flexible as it relates to public funding of religious schools. This will be key in the school voucher cases that the Court will eventually face, and O'Connor does not want to accept that either. This tension becomes clear in two related cases, *Agostini* and *Mitchell*.

Agostini and *Mitchell*

Agostini and *Mitchell* are two Supreme Court cases examining the way that federal money passes through local agencies to schools—for programs in both public and private educational institutions. *Agostini* examined federal money from a Title I program distributed by New York City. *Mitchell* involved federal money distributed by Louisiana under a federal program referred to as "Chapter Two" of the 1981 Federal Education Consolidation and Improvement Act.

In *Agostini*, Justice O'Connor wrote the opinion of the Court arguing that when the federal government channeled money through the Elementary and Secondary Education Act of 1965 to local educational agencies, it was constitutional for those agencies to use funds for all eligible children. This was true whether or not the children attended parochial schools. But, under the program, if money was to go to children who would use the funds in parochial schools, the Title I money had to be used for "secular, neutral and nonideological services" and the services had to "supplement, and in no case supplant, the level of services" already provided by the private school.

O'Connor argued that the assumptions on which earlier cases like *Lemon* relied were still valid.

> For example, we continue to ask whether the government acted with the purpose of advancing or inhibiting religion, and the nature of that inquiry has remained largely unchanged. Likewise, we continue to explore whether the aid has the "effect" of advancing or inhibiting religion. [34]

However, she argued, the Court's understanding of the criteria used to assess whether aid to religion had an impermissible effect had changed.

First, it was no longer true that having a public school teacher on parochial school grounds necessarily results in a problematic symbol of government sponsored religion. It might. But, for O'Connor it all depends on the circumstances. In cases like *Zobrest*, a signer for hearing impaired students was allowed to sign on Catholic school grounds. O'Connor said that even though a signer or interpreter had the opportunity to inject religion or repudiation of religion into the activity of signing, absent evidence of such improper activity the judiciary must trust government agents to act appropriately.

Second, she argued that recently the Court had departed from the rule relied on in earlier cases that all government aid that directly aids the educational function of religious schools is invalid. A type of worldview pluralism is advanced here. In *Witters* a blind person was allowed to use a vocational tuition grant to attend a Christian college.[35] Even though the grant recipient clearly would use the money to obtain religious education, the Court agreed that the tuition grants were made available generally without regard to the sectarian-nonsectarian, or public-nonpublic nature of the institution benefited. As long as the money was available to the student and the student controlled its direction to the sectarian school, the nature of the school, religious or other, did not matter.

O'Connor found that New York City's Title I program did not violate any of three primary criteria used to evaluate whether government aid has the effect of advancing religion:

- it did not result in governmental indoctrination;
- it did not define its recipient by reference to religion;
- it did not create an excessive entanglement.

So, a federally funded program providing supplemental, remedial instruction to disadvantaged children on a neutral basis was not unconstitutional. But, *Agostini* specifically held that this was true when the instruction was given on the premises of sectarian schools in a program containing safeguards requiring the services to be *secular, neutral and nonideological.* The question is, what does this requirement mean?

There are three issues relevant to O'Connor's neutrality approach:

- Who makes the decision to benefit the sectarian institution—the state or the individual? If it is the individual, it is all right.
- Worldview pluralism: when an individual makes the decision, any institution can receive services no matter what worldview, religious or secular.
- The difference between secular and religious: when an agency channels the funds, the plan is constitutional as long as the program ensures the money is used for only secular aspects of the receiving institution.

Agostini demonstrated some confusion between two kinds of neutrality. There is an emphasis on neutrality of worldview—evenhandedness between religion and nonreligion—in that funds are allowed to go to secular and faith-based schools. However, neutrality seems to equal the elevation of secular perspectives over religious perspectives when assessing the nature of services provided. Here, O'Connor does not want government to aid or encourage religious belief. But, if government aids secular belief and not religious, do you still have neutrality? No, not even if you accept the distinction between secular and religious activity in a religious school.

Mitchell came along three years later and it is a perfect example of O'Connor's accommodationism in two respects. Jurisprudential accommodation occurs as O'Connor carefully delineates between the type of programs discussed in earlier school funding cases like *Agostini*, *Mitchell*, *Zobrest*, *Witters*, *Meek*, *Allen* and *Ball*. Behavioral accommodation is demonstrated by her attempt to use a concurring opinion to draw parallels between the plurality conservative branch of the Court and the minority liberal branch. But, *Mitchell* also demonstrates problems with O'Connor's approach to neutrality.

In *Mitchell* Justice Clarence Thomas's plurality opinion asserted that the Court's accepted neutrality principle means only two things. First, it is legitimate to uphold aid that is offered to a broad range of groups or persons without regard to their religion.

> If the religious, irreligious, and areligious are all alike eligible for governmental aid, no one would conclude that any indoctrination that any particular recipient conducts has been done at the behest of government. [36]

Second, it requires asking whether the criteria for allocating the aid create a financial incentive to undertake religious indoctrination.

> Such an incentive is not present where the aid is allocated on the basis of neutral, secular criteria that neither favor nor disfavor religion, and is made available to both religious and secular beneficiaries on a nondiscriminatory basis.[37]

Thomas's approach is clearly worldview pluralism and O'Connor does support it. But, she responded aggressively to Thomas's characterization of what the Court had done over time, saying in essence that Thomas was being an activist—restating the law according to his wishes.

In her concurrence with the result but specific rejection of Thomas's analysis, O'Connor emphasized two things. First, in *Agostini*, neutrality had been only *one* of several factors they considered in determining that New York City's Title I program did not have the impermissible effect of advancing religion.

> In both *Agostini*, our most recent school-aid case, and *Board of Ed. of Central School Dist. No. 1 v Allen*, 392 U.S. 236 (1968), we rested our approval of the relevant programs in part on the fact that the aid had not been used to advance the religious missions of the recipient schools.[38]

They had also relied on three other things:

- the lack of evidence of inculcation of religion by Title I instructors;
- the legal requirement that Title I services be supplemental to regular curricula;
- no Title I funds reached religious schools' coffers.

Second, O'Connor argued that per-capita-aid programs should be treated differently than true private-choice programs. It was important to her that when the government provides aid directly to the student, the student has control over whether the government aid will be applied toward religious education. In that case the fact that aid flows to the religious school and is used for the advancement of religion is wholly dependent on the student's private decision. It is for that reason that in *Agostini*, *Witters* and *Zobrest* the Court rejected the rule that all government aid that directly assists the educational function of religious schools is invalid. When one evaluates government endorsement of religion, the difference between per capita and private choice is important. In O'Connor's opinion the Court had always recognized that special establishment clause dangers exist where the government makes direct money payments to sectarian institutions.

> If, as the plurality contends, a per-capita-aid program is identical in relevant constitutional respects to a true private-choice program, then there is no reason that, under the plurality's reasoning, the government should be precluded from providing direct money payments to religious organizations (including churches) based on the number of persons belonging to each organization. And, because actual diversion is permissible under the plurality's holding, the participating religious organizations (including churches) could use that aid to support religious indoctrination.[39]

She emphasized that approval of New York City's Title I program had rested in part on the lack of evidence of actual diversion of funding to issues related to religious aspects of the private schools' programs. Her real concern is clearly revealed in her discussion about the future. She anticipates the school voucher cases that the Court will eventually have to decide when she observes that

> the plurality opinion foreshadows the approval of direct monetary subsidies to religious organizations, even when they use the money to advance their religious objectives.[40]

But, O'Connor's requirement that government money be used for only the secular, "neutral" aspects of religious education demonstrates her assumptions about the ability of our culture to delineate between what is secular and what is religious. Her assumption bumps up against Thomas's worldview pluralism when they debate the divertability issue.

Before addressing the divertability issue directly, O'Connor explained her approach to the Louisiana Chapter Two program. In rejecting the plurality's rationale, O'Connor demonstrated her neutrality perspective by applying the rules set forth in *Agostini*. *Agostini* asked whether the government acted with the purpose of advancing or inhibiting religion and whether the aid has the effect of doing so. The specific criteria used to determine an impermissible effect have changed over time. Now, she says there are three primary criteria to guide the determination:

- whether the aid results in governmental indoctrination;
- whether the program defines its recipients by reference to religion; and
- whether the aid creates an excessive entanglement between government and religion.

She points out that the parties' objection to the Chapter Two program did not question its secular purpose nor did they contend that it created an excessive entanglement. So, for purposes of deciding whether Chapter Two violated the establishment clause, the Court had to ask only whether the program resulted in governmental indoctrination or defined its recipients by reference to religion. The very same criteria can be reviewed to determine whether a program constitutes a violation of her preferred test—the endorsement of religion.

Her conclusion is that no endorsement exists because

- aid is allocated on the basis of neutral, secular criteria;
- it is supplementary to, and does not supplant, non-federal funds;
- no Chapter Two funds reach the coffers of religious schools;
- the aid is secular;
- evidence of actual diversion is *de minimis*; and
- the program includes adequate safeguards.

You can see the conflicting approaches to neutrality in her list. The first element involves worldview neutrality or worldview pluralism, giving aid to institutions despite the worldview they may promote. However, the fourth element requires the aid to be secular—this is neutrality existing only when secular worldviews are promoted.

O'Connor's primary analytical focus was to ask if Chapter Two resulted in governmental indoctrination. If aid was allocated on the basis of worldview pluralism, if neutral secular criteria were used neither favoring nor disfavoring religion, it was probably all right. She also asked if the aid was made available to both religious and secular beneficiaries on a nondiscriminatory basis. If so, then the program would be constitutional. She found that under Chapter Two, the Secretary of Education allocated funds to the States based on each State's share of the Nation's school-age population. Then, the state educational agency (SEA) of each recipient State distributed the State's Chapter Two funds to local educational agencies (LEA's). The LEA spent money on programs designed to improve student achievement. The statute required that an LEA ensure the "equitable participation" of children enrolled in private nonprofit elementary and secondary schools, and specifically mandated that all LEA expenditures on behalf of children enrolled in private schools "be equal (consistent with the number of children to be served) to expenditures for programs . . . for children enrolled in the public schools of the [LEA]. She concluded that Chapter Two used wholly neutral and secular criteria to allocate aid to students enrolled in religious and secular schools alike. As a result, it created no financial incentive to undertake religious indoctrination.

But, O'Connor then emphasized the importance of the fact that the statute required participating SEA's and LEA's to use and allocate Chapter Two funds only to supplement the funds otherwise available to a religious school. Chapter Two funds must in no case be used to supplant funds from non-Federal sources. This provision ensures that religious schools reap no financial benefit by virtue of receiving loans of materials and equipment. Chapter Two materials and equipment must be "secular, neutral, and nonideological." That restriction is reinforced by a further statutory prohibition on "the making of any payment . . . for religious worship or instruction."

It is here that *divertability* becomes critical. What happens if government aid gets "diverted" to religious aspects or the religious mission of the school? For Thomas divertability was no longer a relevant issue, nor was the sectarian character of a school. As long as the aid was given in a worldview-neutral way, what happened to that aid did not matter. O'Connor, however, took great exception to Thomas's argument that divertability was no longer a concern.

Thomas had said that any tool in a school can be diverted to religious use, so we should have neutral selection criteria for the institutions and should not worry about what happened next. The dissent, led by Souter, said that almost anything can be diverted to religious use so aid should not be given to the school unless the aid was given in the form of tools that absolutely could not be diverted. O'Connor splits the difference between these. She agreed with Thomas that anything can be diverted but it does not necessarily have to be diverted. So, if there is no evidence that diversion has occurred, allow the aid.

The divertability question is complicated because it assumes there is a clear distinction between religious and secular aspects of education. In past cases, the Court had distinguished between different sorts of educational material, saying that diversion of public funds to instructional equipment like computers was not legitimate because computers could be used to extend a religious message. But, government aid lending textbooks was fine because textbooks had a fixed message that could not be diverted to a religious message. Over time, however, most of the justices came to realize that any aid—even lunch—could be used to extend a religious message:

> An educator can use virtually any instructional tool, whether it has ascertainable content or not, to teach a religious message. In this respect, I agree with the plurality that "it is hard to imagine any book that could not, in even moderately skilled hands, serve to illustrate a religious message." . . . For example, even a publicly financed lunch would apparently be unconstitutional under a divertability rationale [like the dissent's] because a religious-school official . . . conceivably could use the lunch to lead the students in a blessing over the bread.[41]

So, O'Connor agreed with Thomas that the tool was not so important but how that tool would be used was critical. She emphasized two things. First, Chapter Two contains both a secular content restriction, and a prohibition on the use of aid for religious worship or instruction. And second, only actual diversion, rather than mere divertability, is constitutionally impermissible.

It is the first of these that illustrates her perspective that good neutrality really means elevating secularism over religious belief. The involvement of government in private, religious schools does not trouble O'Connor as long as that involvement is secular. But, what does it mean to advance the secular but not religious aspects of a religious school? O'Connor is making an assumption about religion—that religion is clearly distinguishable from the secular.

The dissent was troubled by this, arguing that this bifurcated approach to belief would involve government in assessing what is and what is not religious. O'Connor was not troubled by this, but consider what actually took place. At the local level, the Jefferson Parish Public School System (JPPSS) representative met with someone from the nonpublic school and reviewed the way in which the school had used the Chapter Two materials and equipment. The JPPSS representative also randomly selected library books the nonpublic school had acquired through the program. The representative reviewed the books' content to ensure that they complied with the program's secular content restriction and then examined the titles of requested library books, rejecting any book whose title suggested a religious subject matter.

For the dissent, this was untenable: A government employee determines what is inappropriately religious by examining titles? Yes, says O'Connor. Then, the representative ensured that the material was used in classes that had no religious content.

O'Connor's jurisprudence in *Agostini* and *Mitchell* seems to use neutrality in two ways. Worldview neutrality is the foundation of her endorsement test. However, neutrality seems to mean "secular" when she assesses whether federal money supplants other money or whether federal aid is helping to advocate religion. She relies on the secular content restriction of the government statutes but this seems to conflict with the worldview pluralism that she advances when she agrees with Thomas that neutrality means neither advocating nor discriminating against religious belief.

Again, the logical extension of the worldview neutrality perspective in the endorsement test leads to one of two things that O'Connor does not like. In establishment cases it leads to government funding of religious aspects of a school. In free exercise cases it leads to a reduction of the protection religion receives—protection that is denied to nonreligious belief.

The appropriate relationship between government regulation and people's religious or nonreligious belief is a complicated issue. It cannot be developed or understood without paying careful attention to what we mean by these phrases. O'Connor trusts the JPPSS agent and the faith-based schools to have a clear understanding of when religion and religious activity are invoked in a faith-based school and when they are not. This assumption needs careful attention.

Notes

1. I am indebted to Stanley Carlson-Thiess for the articulation of this struggle. At this writing, Carlson-Thiess has an appointment in President George W. Bush's White House, focusing on the partnership between government and faith-based institutions.

2. Stanley Ingber, "Religion or Ideology: A Needed Clarification of the Religion Clauses," *Stanford Law Review* 41 (1989): 233.

3. Ingber, "Religion or Ideology," 285.

4. Ingber, "Religion or Ideology," 285.

5. Roy Clouser, *The Myth of Religious Neutrality* (South Bend, Indiana: University of Notre Dame Press, 1992).

6. Note, "Toward a Constitutional Definition of Religion" *Harvard Law Review* 91 (1978): 1056.

7. Note, "Toward a Constitutional Definition of Religion," 1075, 1076.

8. Ingber, "Religion or Ideology."

9. John Mansfield, "Conscientious Objection—1964 Term," *Religion & Public Order* 9 (1966): 9.

10. Ingber, "Religion or Ideology."

11. Ingber, "Religion or Ideology"; George Freeman, "The Misguided Search for the Definition of Religion," *Georgetown Law Journal* 71 (1983): 1519; Wojciech Sadursky, *Law and Religion* (New York: New York University Press, 1982).

12. Freeman, "The Misguided Search"; Kent Greenawalt, "Religion as a Concept in Constitutional Law," *California Law Review* 72 (1984): 753.

13. Mary Ann Glendon, "Structural Free Exercise" *University of Michigan Law Review* 90 (1991): 549.

14. Robert Alun Jones. *Emile Durkheim: An Introduction to Four Major Work* (Beverly Hills, Calif.: Sage Publications, Inc., 1986): 115.

15. Jones, *Emile Durkheim*, 118.

16. Jones, *Emile Durkheim*, 121.

17. Jones, *Emile Durkheim*, 123.

18. Clouser, *The Myth of Religious Neutrality*, 3.

19. Clouser, *The Myth of Religious Neutrality*, 16.

20. Clouser, *The Myth of Religious Neutrality*, 19
21. Clouser, *The Myth of Religious Neutrality*, 18.
22. Clouser, *The Myth of Religious Neutrality*, 23.
23. Clouser, *The Myth of Religious Neutrality*, 27.
24. Clouser, *The Myth of Religious Neutrality*, 36.
25. Clouser, *The Myth of Religious Neutrality*, 39.
26. Clouser, *The Myth of Religious Neutrality*, 43.
27. Nancy Maveety, *Justice Sandra Day O'Connor: Strategist on the Supreme Court* (Lanham, Md.· Rowman & Littlefield, 1996), 31.
28. Maveety, *Justice Sandra Day O'Connor.*
29. Maveety, *Justice Sandra Day O'Connor.*
30. Maveety, *Justice Sandra Day O'Connor*, 82, 83.
31. *Employment Division v Smith*, 485 U.S. 660 (1990).
32. Maveety, *Justice Sandra Day O'Connor*, 85.
33. *Church of Lukumi Babalu Aye.*
34. *Agostini v Felton*, 521 U.S. 203 (1997).
35. *Witters v Washington Dept. of Services for the Blind*, 474 U.S. 481 (1985).
36. *Mitchell v Helms*, 530 U.S. – No. 98-1648 slip op (2000).
37. *Mitchell*, slip op.
38. *Mitchell*, slip op.
39. *Mitchell*, slip op.
40. *Mitchell*, slip op.
41. *Mitchell*, slip op.

Chapter Seven

Treating Beliefs Equally

This book began with the argument that the definition of religion judges use is integral to their First Amendment religious freedom jurisprudence. If "religion" is belief in God while "secular" means no belief in God, judges will have a narrow reading of the free exercise clause and will interpret the establishment clause to allow a wide range of government support of non-God-related belief systems. However, if "religion" means any ultimate reality and "secular" counts as one of those realities, then judges will have a broad interpretation of both clauses. This means that Scalia's fear expressed in *Smith,* that the legal process will fall apart because so many people will be seeking exemptions to general laws, must be addressed more fully. It also means that our approach to government funding of schools and social service institutions would have to be re-evaluated. Under this approach, the application of the establishment clause would lead us to conclude that all institutions are potentially religious.

The trouble is not that one of these approaches is correct while the other is incorrect. The trouble is that either or both are used intermittently. As judges examine the nature of religious activity, and as they think about what it means to be secular, they are doing so in an environment of complicated assumptions about the nature of religion. These assumptions have to be confronted.

Do We Want to Treat Beliefs Equally?

A government's ability to be neutral toward religion depends on its assumptions about the nature of religious belief. If religion can be substantively defined as belief in God, as requiring belief in extratemporal consequences or as involving worship, it is possible for government to distinguish between religious belief on the one hand and secular, moral or philosophical belief on the other. However, there is still a significant problem because many people argue, and judges recognize, that belief turns action into religious activity. In free exercise cases judges are torn between claiming that the action is secular, often because it is public, and claiming that the action is religious but nonetheless can be controlled. This results in inconsistency in the law. In establishment cases the problem is greater because the nature of establishment clause application is that it involves government, or public action. The difference between secular purposes and religious purposes in establishment clause analysis will be determined by a judge's answer to this question: is religion private or must it, for some, define public social activity?

On the other hand, if, as Clouser argues, all theories are embedded in religion, then the state can be neutral to religion only by treating all belief systems equally—subject to the compelling interest test. The appeal of Clouser's approach is that it releases us from the struggle judges have in separating religious/secular belief, religious/secular activity and religious/secular institutions.

If Clouser is correct that all belief systems are religious in a broad sense, in that they have a concept of the divine, the implications for religious freedom jurisprudence are significant. The idea that all theories are founded in religion means that the only way government can be neutral to religion is to treat all theories (or beliefs or religions) equally. This section considers the way that both the free exercise clause and the establishment clause cases would have to be treated under this type of neutrality.

If government is to be neutral with respect to beliefs we must take an accommodationist approach to free exercise cases. Using Clouser's perspective, the state of free exercise analysis would remain similar to the approach taken by the Supreme Court until 1990 but all sincerely held beliefs would count as "religious." If people claim they should be exempted from laws because of their religious beliefs, they *should* be exempted, subject to the compelling interest test. People claiming moral or philosophical objections to the law should also be exempted, subject to the compelling interest test. This means that if the state passes a law prohibiting use of drugs, it would be no longer just traditional religions that would be exempt from the law. The law would exempt anyone that could articulate a theory or a belief that allowed drug use. The state would of course, face numerous claims that it considers to be suspicious. The state would then have four choices:

- it could get out of the business of controlling behavior, or
- it could evaluate each claim for its sincerity, or

- it could say drug use is such a big problem that there is a compelling interest to restrict drug use in all cases, or
- it could restrict drug use in all cases but some—making certain that the restrictions applied evenhandedly to all beliefs, similar to the "time, place and manner" restrictions currently put on free speech.

Judges who recognize that religious belief is not easily separated from secular belief—or that religious belief has a necessary impact on action—recognize the foundational argument in Clouser's analysis. If we used Clouser's approach we would not have to worry about the difference between religious activity and secular activity, nor would we have to argue about the relationship of faith to the rest of life—public or private. Clouser's approach assumes that all belief is integrally related to life choices.

Establishment clause cases, on the other hand, would require a radically different approach. The current *Lemon* test requires a distinction between religious intent and secular intent by legislators. Clouser's analysis points out that this is a false distinction.

Establishment cases involve government support of certain beliefs; often this support is financial. Clouser's perspective would require that government support be extended to all beliefs equally—again subject to the compelling interest test. So, if government is supporting what we have called "secular" schools, government should also support what we have called "religious" schools. If government is supporting "secular" social service agencies, it should also support "religious" social service agencies.

Resistance to this approach comes in the form of three questions:

1. *What if a belief is harmful to society?* In this case the belief would not require support and could in fact be restricted using the compelling interest test. This is no different from Constitutional analysis in effect today.
2. *Doesn't this system entangle government and religion?* Our current system has not successfully, coherently, guided us on the proper relationship between the state and people or institutions of faith. Part of the problem is that all people are "of faith" under Clouser's understanding of the term. Another problem is that the non-Constitutional term "separation" has led us into a quagmire when we try to distinguish between the terms "secular," "religious," "moral," "philosophical" and "neutral."
3. *How can government support the good life over bad choices under this scheme?* It can't. This scheme assumes that unless there is a truly compelling reason the state should not benefit one belief system over another—even if the majority agrees that one is better. Entanglement currently exists. This approach treats all belief systems fairly—neither elevating nor penalizing what we have traditionally called "religion."

The interesting thing about Clouser's approach is that other democracies are quite active in exploring it to promote choice, social pluralism and participatory democracy. In *The Challenge of Pluralism* Stephen Monsma and Christopher Soper have examined five western democracies' approaches to church-state relations.[1]

In their study, Monsma and Soper consider three different models of church-state relations: a government that promotes "separation of church and state" (the United States), a government that promotes an established church (England) and governments that promote some type of pluralism (Germany, the Netherlands, Australia). After examining the history of church-state relations, the authors look at different public policy issues. They examine general free exercise controversies and they look in detail at the country's willingness to use public funds to pay for faith-based schools and faith-based social service organizations. The following three questions provide a unifying theme in their investigation.

- How far can a democratic polity go in permitting religiously motivated behavior that is contrary to societal welfare or norms?
- Should the state encourage and promote consensual religious beliefs and traditions in an attempt to support the common values and beliefs that bind a society together and make possible limited, democratic government?
- When religious groups and the state are both active in the same fields of endeavor, how can one ensure that the state does not advantage or disadvantage any one religious group or either religion or nonreligion over the other?[2]

After describing the struggles that each country faces, Monsma and Soper make several observations that show how this research can be used to illuminate problems that plague a country like the United States. First, they argue that real governmental neutrality will exist when the right to freely exercise one's faith is limited only by a truly compelling social interest. Second, states cannot be religiously neutral if they insist on trying to promote consensual religious values—those values that are uncontroversial to a majority of the people. Third, strict separation of church and state will result in governmental decisions that discriminate against religious belief—this violates religious neutrality. Fourth, neutrality may at times require policies that actively involve government in funding religious organizations.

The authors' evaluation of the different countries' approaches emerges unapologetically from their belief that the best governments support equally a plurality of worldviews. They believe that the only answer to church-state conflict is to have government policies that treat religious belief and secular belief equally. This genuine neutrality or "evenhandedness" among faiths requires that government accommodate religions when it is accommodating secular belief, and that government aid religious belief when it aids secular belief. Any other approach, they say, ends up favoring secular belief over religious belief and this violates the standard of government neutrality that ought to direct church-state relations.

In a 1998 book, *Equal Treatment of Religion in a Pluralistic Society*, Monsma and Soper drew together constitutional scholars and law professors to discuss different approaches to the treatment of religious belief. Monsma and Soper defined equal treatment of religion as ensuring that

> the establishment clause of the First Amendment . . . is not violated, even if government grants aid, recognition, or support to religion or religious groups, as long as government gives equal aid, recognition, or support to all religions and parallel or similar secularly based systems of belief and their organized groups. Equal treatment, says the First Amendment, does not mandate an artificial, perhaps impossible-to-attain strict separation between government and all of religion in its various manifestations. Instead, it argues that the establishment clause mandates governmental neutrality on matters of religion, a neutrality that is more fully attained by the equal treatment of persons and groups of all faiths—religious and secular—than by an attempt strictly to separate religion and government, which leads to a rejection of all governmental aid, support, and recognition for religious groups.[3]

The approach Monsma and Soper advocate is supported by some of the most prominent Constitutional scholars of our day.[4] Many of the scholars that contributed to the argument in the *Equal Treatment* text, suggested that not only is this sort of equal treatment the best way to handle religious freedom jurisprudence, but that it is the way both the Supreme Court and different legislative acts seem to be leaning in recent years.

Beginning in 1984, the federal government took some serious steps to address the issue of religion in the public arena. The Equal Access Act, passed in 1984, prohibited schools from discriminating against students on the basis of the content of the students' speech. The Act specifically provides that if a school maintains a "limited open forum" during noninstructional time, that forum must be open to all lawful religious, political and philosophical voices.

> It shall be unlawful for any public secondary school which receives Federal financial assistance and which has a limited open forum to deny equal access or a fair opportunity to, or discriminate against, any students who wish to conduct a meeting within that limited open forum on the basis of the religious, political, philosophical, or other content of the speech at such meetings.[5]

The Act applies to any school that qualifies as a secondary school, and it provides that a "limited open forum" occurs when a school allows non-curriculum-related student groups to meet on school premises during noninstructional time.

Generally, it requires that the school apply the same rules and protections to religious students' meetings as it applies to any other non-curriculum-related student meetings. It provides for "equal treatment" of students' speech and activities—whether those activities are considered to be religious, secular or somewhere in between. Then, in 2001, the Supreme Court extended this analysis by finding that the Constitution requires this sort of equal treatment even in elementary schools when after-school programs included worship of God on school ground.[6]

In 1995 and again in 1998, President Bill Clinton took further steps to ensure that public school districts protect religious voices. He directed the Secretary of Education, in consultation with the Attorney General, to inform school districts that according to the Department of Justice and the Department of Education public schools were not to be "religion-free zones." Clinton and the Departments of Justice and Education set forth many principles to supplement the Supreme Court decisions and to guide public schools in their decision-making processes, ensuring that religious speech and belief would be treated fairly.

When in 1990 the Supreme Court handed down the much criticized *Smith* decision, declaring that if a law burdened religious exercise but appeared to be neutral to religion it would be subject to a lower standard of scrutiny, the case produced an outcry by many different groups in society. It resulted in the development of a broadly based coalition of religious and civil rights groups. This coalition worked to develop the Religious Freedom Restoration Act ("RFRA") which said that government may "substantially burden a person's exercise of religion" only if it passes the compelling interest test. The Act gave religious groups greater protection than did the 1990 Supreme Court case; in fact, the Act "restored" the rights of religious persons to the pre-1990 approach to the limitation of Constitutional rights. The Act was passed by the U.S. House and Senate in 1993 and was signed into law by President Bill Clinton in November 1993. However, the law's constitutionality was tested, and in 1997 the Supreme Court declared it to be unconstitutional as applied outside of the federal government. The reason that the Court found the law to be unconstitutional had more to do with federalism and states' rights than with religious freedom jurisprudence. This means that the story of the RFRA is not yet over. The law that was held unconstitutional was a federal law, but the Supreme Court left room for states to develop their own more local versions of RFRA.

In 1996 when the federal welfare program was changed, Congress passed a "Charitable Choice" amendment to the welfare law. Charitable Choice provides that whenever the federal government allows private organizations to assist in the distribution of welfare benefits, the government must also allow religious organizations to have an equal opportunity to participate.

This approach has been ratified by President George W. Bush as he begins his White House Office on faith- and community-based organizations. He argues that faith-based programs need to be partnered with and funded by the government along with programs that identify themselves as secular.

What Really Needs to Happen?

Two problems repeatedly surface as judges try to balance religious freedom concerns: it is commonly assumed that agreement exists on what it means to be "religious," and it is assumed that the "religious" can be separated from the "secular." But, as we try to untangle the implication of these assumptions, we have to spend some time thinking about the job of government as it relates to the beliefs of citizens.

In 1981, a Christian lawyer and political scientist, Bernard Zylstra, wrote an article which outlined various types of rights in a "differentiated" society.[7] Zylstra was Dutch, and he came from a democratic system that worked hard to ensure that government, to the extent possible, would treat all beliefs equally. In a society made up of individuals, the state and institutions, said Zylstra, a just public law must take the identity of each of these into account by ensuring that each entity would have the space to fulfill its role. The task of the state, he argues, is to ensure that citizens have room to function in their other capacities. In order to do this, the state must recognize and enforce protection of the legal identity of a variety of institutions (e.g. churches, schools, families, etc.)

The United States has done a good job in emphasizing the identity and rights of the individual: What is it that makes individuals human? What is it about the humanness of individuals that may not be limited or overcome by the state, or by a majority within the state? The Bill of Rights articulates the limited protections that we have developed. Unfortunately, we have not given sufficient thought to the existence, authority, or rights of other institutions in civil society, and it is at this point that we run into trouble when we talk about "religious institutions" and "secular institutions."

In 1990, Monsma attempted to develop this approach by integrating the rights of these different entities into the fabric of U.S. constitutional law.[8] He labeled his approach "positive neutrality" and it is the foundation for the "equal treatment of religion" that he and Soper advocate. Positive neutrality advances a concept called "structural pluralism"—a phrase that refers to the rights and responsibilities of individual social institutions like families, churches, businesses and the state. It is only after we have an understanding of differentiated responsibilities that we should begin to use concepts popular in U.S. law, like the compelling interest test, to balance conflicting interests between and among individuals or institutions.

Monsma and Zylstra argue in different ways that the inability of Americans to reach political consensus on a wide variety of tough issues could be assuaged if we recognized two things: first, institutions have their own sphere of responsibility, and second, all political perspectives, solutions and desire are grounded in a view of the world and of humanity. This is faith. Therefore, all areas of life, including political solutions, are related to faith. Current policies are not and cannot be religiously "neutral." Because every policy is grounded in a particular view of the world, policy proposals must take into consideration that individuals or institutions that cannot adhere to the government perspective must be acknowledged and accommodated and treated equally to the greatest possible extent.

Consider first the individual. As a Christian Zylstra notes that justice requires a social order in which all people can express themselves as God's image bearers—whether or not they choose to acknowledge God. Justice requires "social space for human personality."[9] Moreover, the right of people to fulfill their callings implies at least three things: the right to be, the right to life itself, and the right to be unharmed. Zylstra develops this by emphasizing the relationship between a person's right to be and the right to believe. A just concept of the state and the individual must accept that people will choose to believe in, and act on their beliefs in, different gods.

> Because of sin, the gods men love are many, and for centuries the lovers of God have denied the right of others to love their god. If in Christ we know what it means to love God, do persons who claim to love God as revealed by Buddha or Mohammed have a right to the fulfillment of their claims? And what about persons who claim that the god they are called upon to love is human personality itself? A just society may not discriminate between one religion and another. The wheat and the tares are allowed to coexist until God's final day of judgment. This does not mean that the society order is neutral with respect to religions. Societal orders ought to be so structured that a multiplicity of religions can flourish side by side.[10]

This approach takes seriously the separation of church and state, but it distinguishes between the concepts "secular" and "religiously neutral." Zylstra seems to say that all people respond in faith to some god. Whether or not they call this "religion," their faith plays a role similar to that of religion. This means that if a state is to treat all faiths equally, or neutrally, it must recognize that even "secular" beliefs are founded on a faith. They are not religiously neutral. To be secular, or to protect the secular, is not religiously neutral. "Neutrality" occurs only when the state grants all faiths, perspectives, worldviews, and ideologies the same credence, financial aid and governmental support.

In addition, institutions need to be free to respond to their calling—whether this calling is God-ordained, or ordained by a sense of people's place in the universe. Monsma's contribution begins with an understanding of a plural order in society, meaning both pluralism of beliefs and pluralism of structures of institutions. He says that religious freedom should extend not only to the "development and practice of a religious structure's core religious beliefs," but also to the development and practice of three other roles of religious associations: molding members' behavior and attitudes, providing services, and influencing the policy-making process.[11] This means that religious freedom not only extends to the beliefs and practices of churches, but should also include the beliefs, activities, and presumably hiring practices of schools, childcare centers and so forth. "A Jewish counseling center should have as full protection for its freedom to act on the basis of its distinctive Jewish character and beliefs as a synagogue. Pluralism insists that the tent of religious freedom be broad enough to encompass all these forms."[12]

Finally, the distinct role of the state must be considered. Both Zylstra and Monsma agree that the state has rights peculiar to it because it has a "unique office." As Christians, Zylstra and Monsma argue that from their perspective the state is God's servant for our good, and its distinctive office is to "establish and maintain a public realm in which the rights of persons and institutions are recognized, protected and guaranteed."[13] But, the fact that the state is God's servant does not mean that those who believe in God should be advantaged. The state is to do justice to *all* beliefs. As Zylstra puts it, the state's responsibility is to acknowledge the rights of individuals, certainly, but also to establish "spheres of freedom within which persons and institutions can exercise rights for the fulfillment of their respective offices, callings and responsibilities."[14]

> The "good" the state is called upon to establish is the salus publica, the public good. This has a variety of implications. In the first place, it means that the state's administration of justice must protect each person within its realm, irrespective of belief, race, class or sex. Each person must be deemed equal before the law of the land. In the second place, the state is a public institution in that its membership, citizenship, must be open to everyone born within its borders. Under no circumstances is the state allowed to annul the citizenship of its members. In the third place, the state is public in that the legal order which it establishes ought to be one in which the spheres of freedom for the nonpolitical institutions and associations are guaranteed and protected from external interference. It must do that in such a way that no person or institution exploits, usurps, or abuses another[15]

The state also has its own sphere of authority.

> The basic right of government is to possess the freedom it needs to exercise an autonomy or sovereignty in its sphere without intervention and interference by other social structures. This means that government has a right to exercise a decision-making authority backed by sanctions. *However, it does not mean that government possesses a full sovereignty that permits it to set society's goals and then limit . . the other structures of society in their pursuit.* Doing so

> would uphold the absolute, and not the quasi-sovereignty of government.[16]

It is the state's role, responsibility and right to make policy that protects and encourages other spheres of authority. But the state does not have the right to set policy that limits the ability of people or institutions to live according to their call—whatever that might be. It is only in rare circumstances that the government can set policy that limits the working out of a belief system.

Taken together, Monsma's and Zylstra's first argument is that religious associations and communities, and their individual members, should not be disadvantaged as they work out their religious beliefs. The second argument is that religious structures, in the exercise of their beliefs and rights, must not transgress on the rights or roles of other spheres, including that of the state.

How can this approach be applied to law within our current Constitutional structure? Interestingly, part of the Title VII case law seems to parallel the concerns of Zylstra and Monsma. Judges do, for the most part, try to acknowledge the institution of the church as an entity having rights. In employment law, the state takes a back seat as it allows what it perceives to be "religious institutions" to define themselves through employment decisions. This is the specific function of the exemptions to Title VII. But questions remain: Which institutions may legitimately make their own decisions regarding their employment practices, and how far should the state go in granting leeway? Is there any point at which the state may step in or oversee the institution's decision? At what point does an institution become accountable to other authorities outside its own sphere?

The problem with current case law is that substantive core conflicts are reflected in the judges' decisions. In some cases, judges impose their own definition of religion, or their own distinction between the religious and the secular, on the litigants. In other cases, the definition of religion is inconsistent with prior court rulings. Again, most of the cases illustrate the inherent conflict between the idea that if something is religious it should be beyond the reach of government control and the reality that religion affects much of life and necessarily has real, social presence. A tension exists between government's desire not to become entangled in the fundamental choices that people make in directing their lives, and government's responsibility, as part of its public justice obligation, to be involved in social life.

The application of Monsma's and Zylstra's approach addresses these problems by articulating a method for distinguishing between government acts that inappropriately limit an institution's identity and government acts which legitimately limit activity. The key tools are the self-identity of the institution and the compelling interest test currently used by the courts to limit government intrusion in areas of citizens' fundamental freedoms.

Self-Identity of Institutions

One problem with case law is that judges are stymied by the problem of defining religion in a way that does not discriminate against groups. They are also confused about what it means to be a religious institution. The cases that explicate the Title VII exemption acknowledge that for some institutions, a broad discretion in the hiring of employees is intrinsic to the goals of the institution. The statute identifies these institutions as "religious" but gives little guidance as to what should be included in this category. The problem is that the very act of categorizing, done by someone outside the institution, can itself be a source of discriminatory definitions of religion. If one's religion is solely defined by rituals and prayer, then one may accept the idea that religion is private and affects only Sunday worship or private life. But if one believes that religion is about ultimate meanings, then religion is a part of everything in life.

Those who believe that their faith defines their lives cannot separate their religious church life from their business life, which is equally religious. The judicial system should not be given the power to determine the religiosity of an organization.

Monsma explains that if religion is a belief system, then it manifests itself and ought to be protected in at least three types of structures. First, religious associations organize the observance of a religious faith and teach its core beliefs.

> In the Christian tradition, formally organized churches, whether on the local congregation or the national denominational levels, are prime examples of this first type of religious association. Synagogues, temples, mosques and other such centers are formal associations that are the equivalent to churches within Christianity. What they all have in common is that they are religious in the sense that they possess a unified system of beliefs and practices that answer ultimate questions by reliance on the supernatural. They are associations in that they are formal organizations with explicit formal structures and usually written statements of faith or purpose.[17]

A second religious structure is an association whose "primary purpose is to provide a structure for the living-out and application in society of a religion's core beliefs."[18] Monsma cites religiously based service organizations such as schools, adoption agencies, hospitals, homeless shelters, and disaster relief agencies as examples. He does not include for-profit business entities in his list, but it is possible for a business to meet this definition as well. The Townley Manufacturing Company, for example, seems clearly to have been established in conjunction with a primary purpose of living out and applying its owners' perspective of the Christian's calling.

A third religious structure is a faith community bound together by "organizing, affective ties, even in the absence of a formal organization."[19] Monsma sees this as a community rooted in ties of "faith, shared traditions, and feelings of self-identity."[20]

All of these structures respond to a calling, and they have the right and responsibility to define themselves in accordance with this calling. But as Monsma describes, positive neutrality and structural pluralism add to the analysis of church-state issues by recognizing and respecting the "quasi-sovereignty" that both the state and religious structures possess in their proper spheres of activity. "Neither the one nor the other grants certain rights or imposes obligations on the other; rather, each possesses certain rights and obligations inherently."[21] This is the key: it is when we understand these identities that we can unravel the complex relationship between religious freedom issues and employment law.

But, how does one draw these parameters? Is there a way to think about the limits on the space of institutions, or the space of government? What happens if a church or other religious institution starts to take on the role of the family or the role of a business? Monsma offers guidance. He says that the essence of institutions' responsibility is respecting the state's exercise of its responsibilities in its appropriate sphere. This involves two things: first, it means accepting the legitimacy of government and obeying its lawful decision. Second, institutions have responsibilities toward society as a whole. They may not interfere improperly in society's other autonomous spheres, such as economics, science, and art. "Churches and other religious associations are not business enterprises, scientific research institutes nor academies of the performing arts and they need to respect the sovereignty of these."[22]

Zylstra adds this limitation on activities of institutions:

> Communities and associations have an identity that is directly dependent upon their office, the service they render society. Their rights are correlative with their office. The right of an institution is its authority to make legally binding decisions for its members pertinent to its office. A society is genuinely free when both persons and institutions can exercise their rights in this sense, without interference by external powers.[23]

The state then, says Monsma, plays its role in regulating institutions by limiting the ability of one institution to interfere with another, and by protecting health, safety, order, and other compelling interests of society. Note the similarity between this approach and the application of the compelling interest test that the Supreme Court uses.

Thus, the rights of an institution are limited by the parameters of its calling and by the rule of noninterference with the roles of other institutions. The role of the state is to protect the space of both individuals and institutions as they work out what it is that they believe they are called to do in this world. The specific application of Monsma's and Zylstra's approaches to the problems of employment law results in a concern for the protection of the self-identity of all institutions, both religious and secular. This includes acknowledging institutions' freedom to make their employment decisions with regard to their self-identity or their identified faith, even if this is completely at odds with the majority's policy concerns regarding race and gender equity. However, because institutions do have responsibilities to individuals and other structures in society, the state does have a role in moderating these relationships.

Monsma seems to suggest that if an act is critical to the identity and purpose of an institution, the act should be protected. The role of the law, then, is to do two things: first, to ascertain the sincerity with which the institution asserts its identity; second, to activate the compelling interest standard to limit only those sincere, self-expressive acts which harm other individuals or structures in society.

If this principle is applied to the cases taken up in the employment law chapter, it becomes clear that neither the accommodationist nor the strict separationist approach is sufficient. Rather than taking a "hands off" approach to the hiring of clergy, and clergy alone, judges should interpret Title VII and the First Amendment to allow all institutions that claim a relationship between their identity and their hiring practices to employ whomever they wish. Institutions do not lose their "religiosity" simply because they operate in the marketplace. For those who believe that faith is integral to all that they do, pastors are not more religious and no more critical to the religious expression of an institution than are Chief Executive Officers or janitors.

By the same taken, however, none of the hiring practices, including the hiring of clergy, should be entirely free from judicial scrutiny. First, institutions should be required to show that their hiring decision does indeed relate to their self-professed identity. Judges should have the right to determine whether or not, in a particular instance, faith precepts are being used as subterfuge for some bias that is not related to the profession of the organization. For example, in those cases where women were denied employment, judges should be able to ask the institutions to prove that gender roles are part of the fiat by which the organization is run. If there is evidence that the organization does not really believe that males must head the organization, or if the question is racial and there is no evidence that the organization has always preached or developed itself in accordance with the separation of the genders or races, then the law should not protect the discriminatory act. Judges should not have the ability to assess the legitimacy of the belief, but they should be able to assess the sincerity and consistency with which the organization truly adheres to the belief.

In cases where past practice shows that gender discrimination or racial discrimination were not part of the belief system or the organization, the practice should not be allowed. In cases where the documents of the organization (its charter, faith statement, articles of incorporation, and bylaws) do not support the claim that gender or race discrimination are part of the belief system, the practice should not be allowed. In cases where past practice and the organization's documents illustrate that discrimination against men or women or people of color are part of the belief system, the practice should be allowed, as long as the state does not have a compelling interest to rule otherwise. In these cases, "compelling interest" must be truly narrowly construed.

The Compelling Interest of the State

The compelling interest test is a standard used in modern Bill of Rights jurisprudence that allowed the government to limit even the fundamental freedoms of American citizens. In some situations, the state believes that it is necessary to limit such rights as free speech, due process, or in this case, religious freedom. The state is allowed to pass laws that limit freedoms only when the state has a compelling interest to do so. A compelling interest usually takes the form of protecting the life or health of citizens. In addition to proving its interest, the state must also prove that it is employing the least restrictive means available to achieve its interest.

It is the compelling interest test that serves as the protective measure to limit acts by institutions that would harm individuals or other institutions in society. If a church or a business claimed that hiring ten-year-olds without pay was part of its self-identity, and this was illustrated by the organization's documents and past practices, the state would still have the right, and the obligation, to intervene and prohibit the practice. The state has a compelling interest in protecting children from exploitation.

Unfortunately, this system is not foolproof. The compelling interest standard can be and has been used to limit the activities of unpopular religions. When judges have to balance the compelling interests of the state and the faith-based institution, they may base their decisions on their own preconceptions about religion and the way children should be brought up. However, if the system begins by recognizing the right of the organization to define itself, and if the organization takes on the responsibility of establishing its belief system and articulating the relationship between its acts and its beliefs, then judges have to be more careful and deliberate when they limit religious expression. They have to state the compelling interest of the government, they are subject to past precedent, and they are subject to being overturned on appeal if their decisions are not carefully documented and argued. This would result in more protection to faith-based organizations than afforded by our current system, which allows judges to circumvent the process by claiming that a belief system is not a religion, or by arguing that an act is secular rather than religious.

If the compelling interest standard is applied to the issue of gender discrimination, governments will argue that they have a compelling interest in eradicating racial and gender discrimination in society. Two arguments, however, belie this approach. First, despite the interest in doing away with discrimination, even the civil rights laws have included exemptions that allow churches to discriminate. This illustrates that as long as the discrimination is circumscribed, and is for an important reason such as allowing another group (often a minority religion) to exist and define itself, society can accommodate the discrimination.

In addition, as long as belonging to a religious group is voluntary, and as long as employment is available outside of a particular faith-based business or organization, people who are discriminated against by the organization have other opportunities. The state's compelling interest argument would be more convincing if it could establish that the faith-based organization had monopolistic control over a particular area of employment, and that potential employees discriminated against by the organization had no other employment options.

This approach does not solve the problem that occurs when people within a faith disagree about that faith's precepts. If some Catholics believe that biblical precepts require priests to be male but other Catholics disagree, the courts have no choice but to stay out of the discussion, in accordance with judicial reluctance to be involved with theological disputes. If judges cannot assess the sincerity of a faith-based organization because there is disagreement in the organization's documents or disagreement among the faith's adherents, the case cannot be handled by the legal system and the employment practices should be allowed to stand.

Churches, church-owned organizations and other faith-based institutions ought to be allowed to work with their employees in accordance with their self-professed ideals. However, they should be held accountable for their decisions. They should be allowed exemptions from general civil rights employment laws, as long as they can establish that their employment policies are truly a part of their belief system.

The same rationale applies to government funding of social service institutions. The fact that a social service institution is thought of as "religious" should not prevent it from receiving funds. All social service institutions emerge from a set of beliefs—and as Clouser would argue, all of these beliefs function as faith. Government should not be selecting one set of beliefs over another in its funding schemes.

However, in like manner, social service institutions that are traditionally considered "religious" should not expect to receive special rights, exempting them from the laws that limit others. This is the key sticking point for many of those that support equal treatment of religion.

Although it is true that Christians lose out on policy issues when they are in the minority, it is also true that many Christians are perfectly willing to use the majoritarian political system to their benefit when they are in the majority. Proponents of equal treatment of religion have often argued on behalf of special exemptions in the law for traditionally religious organizations—even when those exemptions arguably "privilege" religious belief above secular belief.

In *Jimmy Swaggart v Board of Equalization of California* the Supreme Court rejected the argument that the First Amendment required states to exempt religious organizations from the sales taxes that were assessed against general businesses.[24] Several proponents of equal treatment of religion argued on behalf of Jimmy Swaggart Ministries that religious organizations should be treated differently than organizations of other motivation. This sort of argument undercuts the contribution that Monsma and others are trying to make. If the state of California were to exempt non-profit organizations from tax but refused to exempt religious organizations, it would be treating beliefs unequally. However, if it says that all organizations must pay taxes, those organizations that argue for a special exemption because they are "religious" are arguing for unequal treatment of religion.

Curriculum cases under an equal treatment analysis present a slightly different approach. Many European countries have solved this issue by saying that all schools promote values of some sort and all curriculum is based in faith of some sort. Therefore, if the government is going to support schools, it should support all schools equally—both those that we consider state schools and those that we call religious schools. This approach gives full expression to Clouser's perspective that all beliefs rest in religion in the broad sense.

However, it is difficult to imagine that such a radical change could take place any time soon in the United States. It is, on the other hand, easier to think of equal treatment of beliefs within our current public school system. This approach builds on the perspective that the federal legislators and the justices of the Supreme Court took when they applied the Equal Access Act to speech—all speech of students, both that which we call religious and that which we call secular. If we recognized that all curricula are based in a worldview of some sort, public school officials could plan curricula by emphasizing worldview pluralism within the curricula that they structure. To a certain extent we see that now, but in many school districts traditional faiths are left out of the public arena, while in others traditional faiths are happy to dominate the public arena.

If Clouser is correct, then all citizens must be careful to protect the faith expression of all other citizens, subject to a careful and narrow reading of the compelling interest test.

Conclusion

In American society the arguments about the relationship between law, religion and politics seem to be never-ending. Every year hundreds of cases make their way through the courts asking judges to interpret what it really means to have the free exercise of religion while the government refrains from establishing religion. If we want to bring clarity to our case law and our public policy debate, we have to decide if we believe that religion should be treated similarly to other belief or if it should be treated differently. To do that, we have to think through what it means to be religious.

Notes

1. Stephen Monsma and Christopher Soper, *The Challenge of Pluralism* (Lanham, Md.: Rowman & Littlefield, 1997).
2. Monsma and Soper, *The Challenge of Pluralism*, 12.
3. Stephen Monsma and Christopher Soper, *Equal Treatment of Religion in a Pluralistic Society* (Grand Rapids, Mich.: Eerdmans Publishing, 1998), 2.
4. See articles by Carl Esbeck and Michael McConnell in *Equal Treatment of Religion in a Pluralistic Society*.
5. Equal Access Act, 20 U.S.C. 4071-74 (1984).
6. *Good News Club v Milford Central School*, slip op 99-2036 (2001).
7. Bernard Zylstra, "Using the Constitution to Defend Religious Rights," in James Skillen and Rockne McCarthy, *Political Order and the Plural Structure of Society* (Atlanta: Scholars Press, Emory University, 1991).
8. Stephen Monsma, *Positive Neutrality*. (Grand Rapids, Mich.: Baker Books, 1990)
9. Zylstra, "Using the Constitution to Defend Religious Rights," 319.
10. Zylstra, "Using the Constitution to Defend Religious Rights," 319.
11. Monsma, *Positive Neutrality*, 177.
12. Monsma, *Positive Neutrality*, 177.
13. Zylstra, "Using the Constitution to Defend Religious Rights," 320.
14. Zylstra, "Using the Constitution to Defend Religious Rights," 321.
15. Zylstra, "Using the Constitution to Defend Religious Rights," 321.
16. Zylstra, "Using the Constitution to Defend Religious Rights," 321, emphasis added.
17. Monsma, *Positive Neutrality*, 180.
18. Monsma, *Positive Neutrality*, 180.
19. Monsma, *Positive Neutrality*, 181.
20. Monsma, *Positive Neutrality*, 181.
21. Monsma, *Positive Neutrality*, 178, 179.
22. Monsma, *Positive Neutrality*, 185.
23. Zylstra, "Using the Constitution to Defend Religious Rights," 320.
24. *Jimmy Swaggart v. Board of Equalization of California*, 493 U.S. 378 (1990).

List of Cases

Africa v Pennsylvania, 622 F.2d 1025 (3rd Cir. 1981)
Agostini v Felton, 521 U.S. 203 (1997)
Aguilar v Felton, 473 U.S. 402 (1985)
Allegheny County v ACLU, 492 U.S. 573 (1989)
Baz v Walters, 782 F.2d. 701 (7th Cir. 1986)
Bellamy v Mason's, 308 F.Supp. 1025 (1973); aff'd 508 F.2d 504 (4th Cir. 1974)
Bowen v Kendrick, 487 U.S. 589 (1988)
Bowen v Roy, 476 U.S. 693 (1986)
Brown v Dade Christian School, Inc. 556 F.2d 310 (5th Cir. 1977)
Brown v Pena, 441 F.Supp 1382 (S.D. Florida 1977)
Braunfeld v Brown, 366 U.S. 599 (1961)
Cantwell v Connecticut, 310 U.S. 296 (1940)
Church of the Holy Trinity v U.S., 143 U.S. 226 (1892)
Church of the Lukumı Babelu Aye, Inc. v City of Hialeah, Florida, 113 S.Ct. 2217 (1993)
Corporation of the Presiding Bishop of the Church of Jesus Christ of Latter-day Saints et al. v Amos et al., 483 U.S. 327 (1986)
County of Allegheny v American Civil Liberties Union, 492 U.S. 573 (1989)
Daniel v Waters, 515 F.2d 485 (1975)
Davis v Beason, 133 U.S. 333 (1890)
DeNooyer v Livonia Public Schools, 799 F.Supp 744 (E.D. Mich, 1992)
Dettmer v Landon, 799 F.2d 929 (4th Cir. 1986)
Edwards v Aguillanrd, 482 U.S. 578 (1987)
E.E.O.C. v Fremont Christian School, 609 F.Supp. 344 (N.D. California 1984)
E.E.O.C. v Kamehameha School/Bishop Estate, 780 F.Supp. 1317 (D. Hawaii 1991)(reversed on other grounds)

E.E.O.C. v Pacific Press Publishing, 482 F.Supp. 1291 (N.D. California, 1979)
E.E.O.C. v Presbyterian Ministries, Inc, 788 F.Supp 1155 (W.D. Washington, 1992)
E.E.O.C. v Townley Engineering, Inc, 859 F.2d 610 (9th Cir. 1988)
Employment Division, Dept. of Human Resources of Oregon v Smith, 485 U.S. 660 (1990)
Epperson v Arkansas, 393 U.S. 97 (1968)
Everson v Board of Education, 330 U.S. 1 (1947)
Fike v United Methodist Children's Home of Virginia, Inc. 709 F.2d 284 (4th Cir. 1983)
Fleischfresser v Directors of School District, 805 F.Supp 585 (N.D. Ill. 1992)
Forest Hills, 487 F.Supp. 1378 (E.D.Va.1979), reversed and remanded, 642 F.2d 448; 540 F.Supp. 1046, affirmed in part, vacated in part and remanded, 728 F.2d 230; 661 F.Supp. 300, reversed 846 F.2d 260; rehearing denied, cert. denied 109 S.Ct. 837 (1989)
Forte v Coler, 725 F.Supp. 488 (M.D. Fla. 1989)
Founding Church of Scientology of Washington v U.S., 409 F.2d 1146 (D.C. Cir.) cert. denied, 396 U.S. 963 (1969)
Gillette v United States, 401 U.S. 437 (1971)
Goldman v Weinberger, 475 U.S. 503 (1986)
Grove v Mead School Dist. No 354, 753 F.2d 1528 (9th Cir. 1985)
Heffron v International Society for Krishna Consciousness, Inc., 452 U.S. 640 (1981)
Hunt v McNair, 413 U.S. 734 (1973)
International Society for Krishna Consciousness, Inc. v Barber, 650 F.2d 430 (2d Cir. 1981)
Jaffree v Board of School Comm'rs, 554 F.Supp. 1104 (S.D. Ala. 1983), aff'd in part, rev'sd in part, *Jaffree v Wallace*, 705 F.2d 1526 (11th Cir. 1983), cert. denied sub nom. *Board of School Comm'rs v Jaffree*, 466 U.S. 926 (1984); *Jaffree v James*, 554 F.Supp. 1130 (1983) aff'd in part, rev'd in part sub nom. *Jaffree v Wallace*, 705 F.2d 1526 (11th Cir. 1983) aff'd, 472 U.S. 38 (1985)
Jimmy Swaggart v Board of Equalization of California, 493 U.S. 378 (1990)
Kendrick v Sullivan, 766 F.Supp. 1180 (D.D.C.1991)
King's Garden, Inc. v F.C.C. 498 F.2d. 51 (D.C. Cir. 1974)
Kiryas Joel Village School District v Grumet, 114 S.Ct. 2481 (1994)
Lamb's Chapel v Center Meriches, 113 S.Ct. 2141 (1993)
Lemon v Kurtzman, 403 U.S. 602 (1971)
Little v Wuerl, 929 F.2d. 944 (3rd Cir. 1991)
Lynch v Donnelly, 465 U.S. 668 (1984)
Lyng v Northwest Indian Cemetery Protection Assn, 485 U.S. 439 (1988)
Malnak v Yogi, 592 F.2d 197 (3rd Cir. 1979)
Maguire v Marquette University, 627 F.Supp. 1499 (E.D. Wis. 1986)

Marsh v Chambers, 463 U.S. 783 (1983)
Martin v Struthers, 319 U.S. 141 (1943)
McLean v Arkansas Board of Education, 529 F.Supp. 1255 (E.D.Ark.1982)
McClure v The Salvation Army, 323 F.Supp. 1100 (1971); aff'd 460 F.2d 553 (1972)
McCrory v Rapides Regional Medical Center, 635 F.Supp. 975 (W.D. La.1986)
Minnesota Federation of Teachers v. Nelson, 740 F.Supp. 694 (D. Minn. 1990)
Mitchell v Helms, 530 U.S. – No. 98-1648 slip op (2000)
Mozert v Hawkins County Public Schools, 579 F.Supp. 1051 (E.D. Tenn. 1984), 582 F.Supp 201 (1984), reversed and remanded 765 F.2d 75 (6th Cir. 1985)
Murdock v Pennsylvania, 319 U.S. 105 (1943)
O'Lone v Estate of Shabazz, 482 U.S. 342 (1987)
Peloza v Capistrano Unified School District, 782 F.Supp 1412 (C.D. California 1992)
Pierce v Society of Sisters, 268 U.S. 510 (1925)
Pime v Loyola University of Chicago, 803 F.2d 351 (7th Cir.1986)
Rayburn v General Conf. of Seventh-Day Adventists, 772 F.2d 1164 (4th Cir. 1985)
Reynolds v U. S., 98 U.S. 145 (1878)
Roemer v Board of Public Works of Maryland, 426 U.S. 736 (1976)
Salvation Army v New Jersey Department of Community Affairs, 919 F.2d 183 (3rd Cir. 1990)
Scharon v St. Luke's Hospitals, 929 F.2d. 360 (8th Cir. 1991)
Schempp v District of Abington, 374 U.S. 203 (1963)
School District of Abington Township v Schempp, 374 U.S. 203 (1963)
Scopes v State, 154 Tenn 105, 289 S.W. 363 (1927)
Sherbert v Verner, 374 U.S 398 (1963)
Sherman v Community Consolidated District, 980 F.2d 437 (7th Cir. 1992)
Smith v Board of School Comm'rs of Mobile County, 655 F.Supp. 939 (S.D. Ala. 1987), reversed 827 F.2d 684 (11th Cir. 1987)
Thomas v Indiana Employment Security Division, 450 U.S. 707 (1981)
Tilton v Richardson, 403 U.S. 672 (1971)
Torcaso v Watkins, 367 U.S. 488 (1961)
U. S. v Ballard, 322 U.S. 78, 85 (1944)
U. S. v Lee, 455 U.S. 252 (1982)
U. S. v Macintosh, 283 U.S. 605 (1931), overruled on other grounds, 328 U.S. 61 (1946)
U. S. v Robel, 389 U.S. 258 (1967)
U. S. v Seeger, 380 U.S. 163 (1965)
Voswinkel v City of Charlotte, 495 F.Supp. 588 (W.D. North Carolina 1980)
Wallace v Jaffree, 472 U.S. 602 (1985)
Walz v Tax Comm., 397 U.S. 644 (1970)
Welsh v United States, 398 U.S. 333 (1970)
Wessling v Kroger Co. 554 F. Supp. 548 (E.D. Michigan 1982)

Widmar v Vincent, 454 U.S. 263 (1981)
Wisconsin v Yoder, 406 U.S. 205 (1972)
Wright v Houston Independent School District, 366 F.Supp. 1208 (S.D. Texas 1978) aff'd 486 F.2d 137 (5th Cir. 1973) cert. denied 417 U.S. 969 (1974)
Wooley v Maynard, 430 U.S. 705 (1977)
Zobrest v Catalina Foothills School District, 113 S.Ct. 2462 (1993)

Bibliography

Baer, Richard. "They Are Teaching Religion in the Public Schools." *Christianity Today* (Feb. 17, 1984): 12.

Carter, Stephen. *The Culture of Disbelief: How American Law and Politics Trivialize Religious Devotion*. New York: Harper Collins, 1993.

Caudill, David. "Law and Worldview: Problems in the Creation-Science Controversy." *Journal of Law and Religion* 3 (1985): 1.

Clouser, Roy. *The Myth of Religious Neutrality*. South Bend, Indiana: University of Notre Dame Press, 1992.

Freeman, George. "The Misguided Search for the Definition of Religion." *Georgetown Law Journal* 71 (1983): 1519.

Glendon, MaryAnn. "Structural Free Exercise." *Michigan Law Review* 90 (1991): 477.

Glenn, Charles. *The Myth of the Common School*. Amherst, Mass.: University of Massachusetts Press, 1988.

Greenawalt, Kent. "Religion as a Concept in Constitutional Law." *California Law Review* 72 (1984): 753.

Ingber, Stanley. "Religion or Ideology: A Needed Clarification of the Religion Clauses." *Stanford Law Review* 41 (1989): 233.

Jones, Robert. *Emile Durkheim: An Introduction to Four Major Works*. Beverly Hills, Calif.: Sage Publications, Inc., 1986.

Laycock, Douglas. "A Survey of Religious Liberty in the United States." *Ohio State Law Journal* 47 (1986): 409.

Laycock, Douglas. "Towards a General Theory of the Religion Clauses: The Case of Church Labor Relations and the Right to Church Autonomy." *Columbia Law Review* 81 (1981): 1373.

Mansfield, John. "Conscientious Objection, 1964 Term." *Religion & Public Order* 9 (1966): 246.

Maveety Nancy, *Justice Sandra Day O'Connor: Strategist on the Supreme Court*. Lanham, Md.: Rowman & Littlefield, 1996.

McCarthy, Rockne, James W. Skillen and William A. Harper. *Disestablishment a Second Time: Genuine Pluralism for American Schools*. Grand Rapids, Mich.: Christian University Press, 1982.

McConnell, Michael. "Free Exercise Revisionism: The Smith Decision." *University of Chicago Law Review* 57 (1990): 1109.

McConnell, Michael. "Neutrality Under the Religion Clauses." *Northwestern University Law Review* 81 (1986): 146.

McConnell, Michael. "The Religion Clauses of the First Amendment: Where is the Supreme Court Heading?" *Catholic Law Review* 32 (1989): 187.

Mead, Sidney. *The Lively Experiment*. New York: Harper & Row, 1965.

Melton, James. *A Directory of Religious Bodies in the United States*. City: Press, 1977.

Monsma, Stephen. *Positive Neutrality*. Grand Rapids, Mich.: Baker Book House, 1991.

Monsma, Stephen and Christopher Soper. *The Challenge of Pluralism*. Lanham, Md.: Rowman & Littlefield, 1997.

Monsma, Stephen and Christopher Soper. *Equal Treatment of Religion in a Pluralistic Society*. Grand Rapids, Mich.: Wm. Eerdmans, 1998.

Neuhaus, Richard, ed. *Democracy and the Renewal of Public Education*. Grand Rapids, Mich.: Wm. Eerdmans, 1987.

Noonan, John. *The Lustre of our Country*. San Diego, Calif.: University of California Press, 1998.

Note, "Toward a Constitutional Definition of Religion," *Harvard Law Review* 91 (1978): 1056.

Sadursky, Wojciech. *Law and Religion*. New York: New York University Press, 1982.

Tipton, Stephen. "Republic and Liberal State: The Place of Religion in an Ambiguous Polity." *Emory Law Journal* 39 (1990) 191.

Tushnet, Mark. "The Constitution of Religion." *Connecticut Law Review* 18 (1986): 701.

Weber, Paul. *Private Churches and Public Money*. Westport, Conn.: Greenwood Press, 1981.

Witte, John. "How to Govern a City on a Hill: The Early Puritan Contribution to American Constitutionalism," *Emory Law Journal* 39 (1990): 41

Zylstra, Bernard. "Using the Constitution to Defend Religious Rights." In *Political Order and the Plural Structure of Society*, ed. James Skillen and Rockne McCarthy. Atlanta: Scholars Press, Emory University, 1991.

Index

About the Author

Julia K. Stronks is an attorney and has a Ph.D. in political science from the University of Maryland. She has written numerous articles on the relationship between faith and public policy, and she is the coauthor of the book *Christian Teacher in Public Schools*. She is currently a professor of political science at Whitworth College in Spokane, Washington, where she lives with her husband and her son.

www.ingramcontent.com/pod-product-compliance
Ingram Content Group UK Ltd.
Pitfield, Milton Keynes, MK11 3LW, UK
UKHW012041150926
475560UK00001B/129

9 780739 103128